THE
SIERRA CLUB

A HANDBOOK

Edited by

DAVID R. BROWER

Editorial Committee for the Handbook
ANSEL ADAMS, WILLIAM E. COLBY, FRED GUNSKY,
CHARLOTTE E. MAUK, HARRIET T. PARSONS, BLANCHE STALLINGS

SIERRA CLUB · SAN FRANCISCO · 1960

Preface

Aᴍᴇʀɪᴄᴀ's resources of scenery that we explore and enjoy today are not set aside through accident. National parks and forests, state and county redwood groves and beaches, wilderness areas and primeval regions—these are not now open to free public enjoyment just through happenstance, just because the country is so big and its resources so limitless that no one has yet got around to fencing them in.

These areas, to which millions go each year for escape, exercise, or rest, are available only because men have fought for them. We who enjoy the mountains today owe a debt to generations of men now gone, or now no longer able to be fully active, who have thought in terms of long-range public use and enjoyment rather than immediate development and exploitation. The people of America owe to these men of vision much of what we most enjoy—the national parks, the preservation of some of the redwoods, the recreational areas of the national forests, whether set aside as wilderness or opened to controlled roadside development, the unfenced beaches, the national monuments, the county and city parks.

Opposed to the men of vision there have always been some too-enterprising men of commerce, who have been slow to comprehend that the retention of outstanding scenic and recreational areas as public domain is good business in the long run—who are forever seeking the lever with which to move the earth, and who in their commercial role hear only today's ring of the cash register.

The campaign between men of vision and the cash-register men has been long. Where the men of vision have lost battles, we see unpleasant things when the dust of battle settles. We see the flood where there used to be the scenic masterpiece of Hetch Hetchy Valley, drowned for a purpose which other valleys, not scenic masterpieces, would have served better. We see many a sylvan dell in the mountains, and many an acre of rich agricultural land dredged inside out, with heaps of debris left as monuments to false economy—the saving of the few cents a ton which would have leveled off the piles of boulders and given nature a chance to build soil again. We see inadequate metropolitan zoning, sewage dumped into waters the shore of which could otherwise rival the Riviera. We see all-but-ageless Big Tree stands blasted down for fenceposts and grape stakes (the fragments being hardly good for anything else). We have seen wasteful logging methods that have given too little thought to a recurrent yield, and we're still seeing them. We've seen a bonanza-like salmon run reduced to insignificance, herds of sea otters stoned and skinned, mountain meadows irreparably damaged to produce a few extra pounds of meat. We've seen a race to pump up oil—a resource that will not be replaced in this civilization's time or that of many civilizations to come—by halfway methods for extravagant use. To look at the scene in its most terrible implication, we can see that men of one generation's time—the generation that saw two world wars—have "developed" (that is, have used up) more of the earth's resources than all preceding generations of all known civilizations.

It is far too late now to advocate, even if we would, a return to the tepee—to the Indian's custom of living on the income of natural resources, the replenishable deer, acorns, pine nuts, and grasshoppers. It's too late to urge that we quit our present-day habit of squandering large portions of a bountiful natural endowment of resources (thinking ourselves incomparably clever and enterprising as we admire the gain of the moment).

No, we won't return voluntarily to the tepee. Our descendants can live there later, when the inevitable eviction notice is served.

But we can be cognizant of the conflagration to which we are contributing our small part, and think hard before we stoke the flames now consuming the resources of a land which those resources have made great.

In thinking twice, we can look more carefully at our own chosen field, conservation as it applies to the natural scene. We can thank the men who have handed down to us such mountain recreation lands as we now enjoy. We can realize that our debt can never be paid to them. We can be reasonably sure that they would thank us, and consider the debt well paid, if we took care of the unspoiled places they saved for us, if we didn't overgraze, overlumber, overmechanize, overski them, but passed them on with as few scars as possible to their grandchildren.

Each day, whether in Congress, in state legislatures, or in a park or a forest, some new challenge presents itself, and someone must take the conservative role of the conservationist in accepting that challenge. In this handbook the member who seeks it can discover his own role, a chance to apply the initiative required for checking those who would squander resources that should be saved for tomorrow.

Yes, a debt to the past becomes a debt to the future. In our own field, each pleasant day in mountains should perhaps be charged against us; our account should then be credited for each day on which we extend our vision and give a nod to posterity—on which we act for the unnumbered men who will have to be less prodigal than we and who are entitled to explore and enjoy mountains as pleasant as ours.

The challenge to conserve is best met by those who know and love that which they are called upon to save. To this end, the Sierra Club has always sponsored appropriate activities. These pages, then, give the form and function of the Sierra Club. They tell what it is—what the principal activities of its members are and how they have developed. They tell what the club has done, relying upon members who may have entered the club primarily to participate in physical activities, but whose interest far outlasted any mere physical participation. Finally, these pages will imply what the Sierra Club can do in the years to come. It is hoped that all members, in knowing more fully what the club is, can thereupon increase its value to them and theirs to it and to its cause.

◇

The editor and the committee express their appreciation—

To those who have written the articles and sections: William E. Colby on the history; Ansel Adams for many photographs, and words about the meaning of mountains; August Frugé on publications; Francis Farquhar on place names; Alex Hildebrand on lodges and lands; Harriet Parsons on mountaineering; Lewis F. Clark on winter sports; Walter A. Starr on trails; John Thomas Howell on science; Charlotte E. Mauk on motion pictures; Alfred E. Weiler on the library; Walter L. Huber on bequests; Blanche Stallings for the compilation of folklore; Richard M. Leonard, Charlotte Mauk, and the Outing Committee for the compilation of outing data; the late Marion Randall Parsons for her interpretation of purposes.

To John P. Schagen for the sketches and maps about lodges.

To Oxford University Press for the quotations from *Round River*, by Aldo Leopold.

To the officers and members who long ago conceived of a handbook and who will supply the suggestions that make the next edition more useful; to Anne Brower, the Editor's editor.   D. R. B.

Prefatory note to fifth printing: The first printing of the Handbook appeared as the November 1947 issue of the *Sierra Club Bulletin.* In 1951, with the help of Blanche Stallings, the first printing was revised and brought up to date and was issued as a separate publication. It included a new article on Muiriana by William E. Colby and a revision of "The Sierra Club and Science" by Milton Hildebrand. The *Handbook* was revised and brought up to date again, with the assistance of Blanche Stallings and Fred Gunsky, in 1955; that revision lasted only two years and gave the editor a chance to add new chapters about the club's national activity and conservationist role. The number of changes in this printing demonstrates that the Sierra Club is anything but static. D. R. B.

CONTENTS

THIRTY-TWO PAGES OF PLATES

About Purposes

THE PURPOSES of the Sierra Club, as first stated in the Articles of Incorporation, were: to explore, enjoy and render accessible the mountain regions of the Pacific Coast; to publish authentic information concerning them; to enlist the support and coöperation of the people and the Government in preserving the forests and other natural features of the Sierra Nevada.

The half century after the Sierra Club was founded marked so great a change in the problems affecting the Sierra Nevada that some restatement of purposes became advisable, and the By-Laws were amended to read as follows: to explore, enjoy, and preserve the Sierra Nevada and other scenic resources of the United States and its forests, waters, wildlife, and wilderness; to undertake and to publish scientific, literary, and educational studies concerning them; to educate the people with regard to the national and state forests, parks, monuments, and other natural resources of especial scenic beauty and to enlist public interest and coöperation in protecting them.

The Pacific Coast mountains, at one time known only to a handful of people and open to every form of exploitation, have now been explored thoroughly, indeed exhaustively, by geologists, geographers, biologists, botanists, hikers, mountaineers, skiers, rock climbers. And as for other aims, to "enjoy" and to "render accessible" all too rapidly became incompatible terms. The automobile, advancing roads, the increase in population, all constitute a growing threat to the wilderness areas that the Sierra Club has pledged itself to keep unspoiled for future generations.

The creation of a national or a state park does not necessarily nullify this threat; rather the added amount of travel directed there may even increase it—rightly so in some reserves, such as Yosemite, where the widest possible attendance is implicit. But to preserve a mountain area in its primitive state means a certain amount of restriction in its use, even by pack-mule campers. Roads, hotels, motor boats, ski lifts—none of the trappings of "improved" vacation areas have a place here, and only strictly limited developments indispensable to its best use should be allowed to gain a foothold.

The need everywhere for additional recreational facilities is beyond dispute, but this fact must not be allowed to confuse the fundamental issue. It is a far cry from Coney Island or the Russian River to Point Lobos or the Kings-Kern Divide, yet all of these recreation spots have their addicts. New vacation centers must be created to meet the needs of either taste—but not in the same place. The Coney Islands are on the increase; our glacial canyons, our redwoods and rhododendron gardens are yearly menaced by some new encroachment, all too often in the alleged interest of some special group or sport.

To keep our small remaining wilderness areas unharmed, for the enjoyment of generations after ours, our constant vigilance and our most earnest efforts must be turned toward "developing" these areas only in such ways as may give them maximum use with minimum damage, which is to say with the fewest possible artificial modifications or commercial concessions. Our policy is, as it always has been in the past, to confer with and advise the administrative agencies which determine the use of these areas; to publicize and do our utmost to avert all threats to their integrity. And within our own membership to keep constantly in mind that no one activity or interest of the club can ever be allowed to take precedence over its fundamental purposes.

CONSERVATION—AND TINKERING

CONSERVATION is a state of harmony between men and land. By land is meant all of the things on, over, or in the earth. Harmony with land is like harmony with a friend; you cannot cherish his right hand and chop off his left. . . .

The outstanding scientific discovery of the twentieth century is not television, or radio, but rather the complexity of the land organism. Only those who know the most about it can appreciate how little we know about it. The last word in ignorance is the man who says of an animal or plant: 'What good is it?' If the land mechanism as a whole is good, then every part is good, whether we understand it or not. If the biota, in the course of aeons, has built something we like but do not understand, then who but a fool would discard seemingly useless parts? To keep every cog and wheel is the first precaution of intelligent tinkering.

—ALDO LEOPOLD, in *Round River* (Oxford, 1953)

The Story of the Sierra Club

The story of the Sierra Club is here most fittingly told by the man who with unfailing devotion has served it for more than half a century. In telling that story, however, William E. Colby characteristically has omitted one prime factor in the club's success—his own unparalleled service-record. Forty-nine years as a director, forty-four as secretary, thirty-six as chairman of the Outing Committee, nine on the State Park Commission—a "volunteer's" contribution to the assets of his country that it would be hard to equal anywhere. Yet beyond these more readily evaluated services his associates bear grateful witness to those qualities of selflessness, of unassertive yet firm leadership, of high idealism and unswerving adherence to its best purposes, that long have made membership in the Sierra Club so memorable a part in so many lives.—M.R.P.

THE GREAT Range of Light noted on the maps as the Sierra Nevada is not only one of the most inspiring and hospitable mountain ranges in the whole world but it has among its manifold attractions the noblest individual trees, the grandest forests in the world, and many incomparable Yosemite-like canyons. It was inevitable that some group of people who held scenes like these in high esteem would become associated in the common cause of protecting the irreplaceable values of the Sierra from ravages of the greed which unfortunately accompanies the advance of civilization. The Sierra Club, born of such a group, assumed this difficult task, and for more than half a century has been fighting the good fight to preserve a priceless heritage of scenic beauty in the Sierra and other American mountain regions as well.

It was a young Scotsman, John Muir, who grew up in the wilderness frontier of Wisconsin and came to California in 1868, who early recognized the importance of saving some of the primitive grandeur he found in California in such abundance. This is especially remarkable when we recall that he began preaching for the wilderness while the West was still in its pioneer days—while forests and rugged scenery were, to the pioneers, little more than a formidable, sometimes hazardous barricade. He had vision.

Muir began to earn his living in California by tending sheep near Merced, and accompanied a large flock into the Tuolumne Meadows in 1869. Ardent lover of flowers and trees that he was, he noted the destructive effects of those "hoofed locusts" on the wild gardens and forests through which they passed. In 1889 he took Robert Underwood Johnson, one of the editors of *Century Magazine,* up into this High Sierra region; around a campfire in the Tuolumne Meadows, they resolved to remedy this devastation. Muir wrote descriptive articles for the *Century Maga-zine,* calling attention to the necessity for protective legislation. Johnson, who had a wide congressional acquaintance, had a bill introduced in Congress which in 1890 created the Yosemite National Park. This em-braced the headwaters of the Merced and Tuolumne rivers and sur-rounded the Yosemite Valley, then a state park, which in 1864 had been turned over to California for safe keeping. This bill was passed so expedi-tiously that the park was created before many people in California real-ized what had been done. As soon as the full import of the Act was recog-nized and it was realized that sheep and cattle could no longer lawfully enter on public land within its borders, the stockmen, who had been reap-ing a rich harvest at public expense without paying a cent of rental for grazing their flocks and herds on these lands, rose up in indignation and used every effort and political device to have the park abolished, or at least materially reduced in area. It took strenuous work on the part of those responsible for the creation of the park successfully to resist these powerful and persistent assaults. Johnson wrote to Muir suggesting that he form an association in California of like-minded men who would as-sume some of the burden of resisting these attacks, which Johnson recog-nized would be repeated as long as there was any chance of breaking down park boundaries.

The formation of an organization of this sort had been in the minds of many who loved the out-of-doors, but it remained for some one to take the initiative. John Muir was unsurpassed in the role of a prophet preach-ing the gospel of wildness and urging its preservation, but he was not an organizer. Professor J. H. Senger, of the University of California, how-ever, was an organizer. As early as 1886 he thought of establishing a mountaineering library in Yosemite Valley. In 1890 he discussed at the University a plan for forming an association of those interested in moun-tain travel; the name "Sierra Club" was suggested for such an organiza-tion. Early in 1892 Senger interested Warren Olney, an attorney promi-nent in Oakland and San Francisco, in his plan of forming "a Sierra Club." He evidently wrote to John Muir to enlist his support, for on May 10, Muir replied that he was "greatly interested in the formation of an Alpine Club and think with you and Mr. Olney that the time has come when such a club should be organized. You may count on me as a member and as willing to do all in my power to further the interests of such a club."

On May 22 he wrote Senger, "I will gladly attend the meeting on Saturday next at Mr. Olney's office [and hope] that we will be able to do something for wildness." On Saturday, May 28, 1892, in Olney's law office in San Francisco, the club's name and purposes were agreed upon, and Olney drew up the Articles of Incorporation. One week later the Articles and the By-Laws were signed and the officers of the club were elected. There were 182 charter members.

The first directors were John Muir, President; Warren Olney, Vice-President; William Dellam Armes, Secretary; J. H. Senger, David Starr Jordan (president of the new Stanford University), Robert M. Price, Mark Brickell Kerr, Willard D. Johnson, and John C. Branner (later president of Stanford). Muir remained president until his death on December 24, 1914. From the outset both universities, California and Stanford, were represented on the Board, and for many years thereafter much of the strength and initiative of the club came from their faculties and student bodies. Many other prominent names appear as signers of the Articles, among them William H. Beatty, Chief Justice of the Supreme Court of California; George C. Perkins, United States Senator; W. L. Jepson, California's outstanding authority on its trees and flowers; and Will Denman, now the senior judge of the United States Court of Appeals.

Samuel Merrill, who was staying at the time at the Muir home in Alhambra Valley, writes that when John Muir returned from that organization meeting he had "never seen Mr. Muir so animated and happy."

As soon as the club was created it began its good work by vigorously and successfully opposing serious efforts to reduce by one half the area of the Yosemite National Park. The club also held public educational and scientific meetings; at one of these, in the fall of 1895, Muir, Professor Joseph LeConte, and Professor William R. Dudley spoke in favor of establishing national forest reservations, later called national forests. Because of forward-looking action on the part of the club, California was the first western state to welcome and have extensive national forests established within its borders. John Muir had much to do with this work and served on one of the early national forest commissions appointed by President Cleveland to make field investigations and recommendations on this subject.

Many of the Sierra Club members were pioneers in the exploration of the theretofore little known and less accessible regions of the High Sierra. John Muir was preëminent in this. Professor J. N. LeConte and Theodore S. Solomons did much writing and pioneer mapping.

The club has at various times, especially during its earlier days when trails were poor and few, contributed funds toward trail building and improvement. It was the chief motivator of the John Muir Trail, constructed by the state as a memorial to John Muir. The club has also contributed toward the purchase of lands and property and has been instrumental in their donation to the federal government, notably the Tioga Road and Power's property at Lake Tenaya in Yosemite National Park, and Redwood Meadows and other important holdings in Sequoia National Park. Much of this was done during the regime of Stephen Mather, the first director of national parks, also a loyal and enthusiastic member of the club, who gave generously of his personal fortune and energy in advancing national-park interests.

The club's first headquarters were in a cubbyhole in the Academy of Sciences building, on Market Street. Public educational and scientific meetings were held in the auditorium of this building. In 1898 the club moved to the Merchants Exchange Building, where it shared offices with the Geographical Society of the Pacific. Colorful Professor George Davidson was president of the latter and also a director of the club. In 1903 the headquarters were moved to a large, well-lighted room in the Mills Building, where for the first time the club's maps, books, and photographs could be appropriately displayed. With the exception of the brief interlude occasioned by the San Francisco earthquake, the principal headquarters of the club continued to be in the Mills Building until they were moved to the adjacent Mills Tower.

In 1905 the By-Laws were amended to provide for the organization of sections, or chapters, thus giving local groups more autonomy and opportunity to act in matters of local importance. The Southern California (now Angeles) Chapter was formed on a permanent basis in 1911 and it has since grown to major importance with headquarters at the Los Angeles office of the club, 427 West Fifth Street. Since then these chapters have been formed: San Francisco Bay (1924), Riverside (1932), Loma Prieta (Santa Clara Valley, 1933) Mother Lode (Sacramento Valley, 1939), San Diego (1948), Atlantic (New York area, 1950), Kern-Kaweah (southern San Joaquin Valley, 1952), Los Padres (Santa Barbara area, 1952), Tehipite (northern San Joaquin Valley, 1953), Pacific Northwest (1954), and Toiyabe (Great Basin, 1957). The chapters are primarily concerned with local activities and problems, such as week-end outings, educational and scientific lectures, reunions, and dinners, and are of great value in studying the facts on conservation problems in their areas.

The outstanding work of the club has been in aiding in the creation of national parks and wilderness areas and in the educational work in preserving them when once created. The successful efforts to keep Yosemite boundaries intact have been mentioned. That was but the first of many

Yosemite problems. The second came soon. John Muir, who had spent many years in the Yosemite Valley, became convinced that the valley was poorly managed by state authorities, both because the state appropriated too little for its upkeep and because the State Commissioners were, except at the outset, selected for purely political reasons and seldom had any adequate concept of what the park was for. In 1903, when Muir accompanied President Theodore Roosevelt on a pack trip in the region, he broached the possibility of having the valley returned to the United States and included in the surrounding national park. The President at once recognized the logic of such a transfer and George C. Pardee, then Governor of California, who was also consulted, agreed that it would be a wise move. As the result of state and federal legislation, the recession was accomplished. It is quite certain that without the work that the Sierra Club did, the local and even national political prejudices could not have been overcome. Whereas the state had been spending a paltry sum each year and the valley was in consequence poorly administered, the federal government has appropriated far more adequately and has done a splendid job of administration. The club's existence would be amply justified by its role in this one controversy.

Another great battle involving Yosemite arose shortly after; in 1906, the City of San Francisco renewed its application, previously denied, for permission to dam Hetch Hetchy Valley, one of the outstanding scenic features of the park, in order to use the stored water for its municipal water supply. In this fight the club was torn internally, for many of its members favored the plan, and among them were important city officials. However, on a test, the club members voted overwhelmingly to oppose this unnecessary invasion of the park. The club took the position that, since it was admitted that good water could be obtained elsewhere, even though at increased cost, the destruction of such an outstanding asset of the park as Hetch Hetchy Valley and the establishment of such a precedent, so dangerous to the whole national-park idea, was not justified. For a time, particularly because of the close friendship which existed between Muir and President Theodore Roosevelt and later President Taft, the club was able to stave off the attack on Hetch Hetchy Valley and divert any concession to the much less important Lake Eleanor and Cherry River region. But political affairs in Washington took a sudden turn and, over the vigorous opposition of the club and its friends, the destructive grant was authorized. Subsequent events have proved the club to have been thoroughly right in its attempt to save the park from this violation of its integrity. Ample water has been shown to have been obtainable elsewhere, and the charge made by the club that what San Francisco really wanted was not so much the water as it was the free water power which was then available—free only because the foresight of Muir and others in creating the Yosemite National Park had preserved Hetch Hetchy from earlier appropriation. It had been thought safely protected by its inclusion in a national park. While this particular battle was lost, the vigorous opposition of the club aroused the entire country to the dangers menacing our parks and it has deterred others from attempting similar inroads. The prestige of the club was enhanced immeasurably.

Still another outstanding accomplishment was the creation of the Kings Canyon National Park in 1940. John Muir had recommended setting aside this area long before the turn of the century. Efforts had been made on various occasions to bring this about, but they had all failed with the exception of one which was partly successful in that it added the upper Kern River region, including Mount Whitney, to the Sequoia National Park. This was sponsored by the Sierra Club, and it was on its recommendation to Stephen Mather, Director of National Parks, that it was decided to add the Kern region to the existing Sequoia Park and to abandon temporarily the effort to include the High Sierra region of the Kings until a more propitious day. This time arrived when Secretary of the Interior Ickes made a special trip to the West Coast to enlist the support of the Sierra Club in urging the creation of the Kings Canyon National Park. The proposed park boundaries were carefully drawn, mainly as the club had suggested. Powerful opposition arose and it was largely because of the convincing illustrated literature that was sent out by the club and like organizations that the area was saved as a national park. Secretary Ickes wrote that it was very doubtful whether the park could have been created without the club's help.

A milestone in the life of the Sierra Club was the inauguration of its annual outings, which began in 1901. At the outset many of the directors were dubious about the advisability of such a radical move, largely because it might involve the club in financial difficulties. However, John Muir was heartily in favor of the plan because it would accomplish what he had devoted his life to preaching—getting people to go out and enjoy these incomparable wilderness areas—and his advocacy prevailed. The club had two interrelated objectives in view—to increase its membership (these outings were limited to members and their immediate kin) and to educate its members and convince them of the importance and necessity of preserving for all time these irreplaceable values. The outings proved a success from the very start, and were amply justified by the results. It is doubtful whether the Sierra Club would have become such a potent force in accomplishing much that it later advocated with such success, without the effective backing of its large, enthusiastic, well-informed membership. A large part of the club's power and influence has been clearly attributable to the indirect benefits of these outings. They have alternated among the Yoesmite, Kings, and Kern High Sierra regions; a few have been taken to Mount Rainier, Glacier, and Yellowstone national parks, and some have visited national parks in Canada. As a result of these outings, hundreds of persons each year have visited high mountain areas that it would otherwise have been very difficult for them to reach. In 1956 there were 27 outings in several Western states.

In addition, countless minor excursions lasting two or more days have been taken by the various sections under club auspices, to points of interest including the Grand Canyon, the desert areas, Mounts Shasta and Lassen, and each year over Decoration Day several hundred members visit Yosemite Valley. These trips blend into the local walks conducted by each club chapter, which are held every week end throughout the year and which afford a splendid companionable opportunity for advancing the cause of conservation and for study of natural history.

Another activity which has attracted many members is skiing. Enthusiasts in this outdoor sport, so closely related to mountaineering, now constitute a large portion of the membership. Clair Tappaan Lodge and Keller Peak and San Antonio ski huts have given members an opportunity to ski at modest expense, for the overnight accommodations are financed on a mutual basis without any idea of profit. This activity has increased the membership materially. Winter sports and lodges are discussed more fully elsewhere in these pages.

The club has, in the face of powerful opposition, resisted encroachments on national parks, favored the creation of national forests, including the more recently created Appalachian National Forest; aided in the creation of Glacier, Estes Park, Grand Canyon and other national parks; and was primarily instrumental in the setting aside of the Devils Postpile National Monument. It has contributed to the purchase of private lands in national parks, which were then donated to the government; assisted in the passage of the bill creating the National Park Service; contributed to the purchase of redwood lands which have been included in state parks; and coöperated with the Save-the-Redwoods League in creating state parks and in preserving them from encroachment. It has opposed the desecration of regions set aside as wilderness areas; aided in the stocking of fishless waters of the Sierra with trout.

The club has aided and advocated the interpretive programs in national parks, and helped inaugurate the Yosemite School of Field Natural History, the geological studies in Yosemite by François E. Matthes, and the studies of animal life in the Yosemite by Joseph Grinnell and Tracy I. Storer; it has urged the construction of trails, and the strengthening of legislative, regulatory and administrative protection of the superlative regions that the Sierra trails have made it possible for people to enjoy and explore; it has advocated comprehensive studies to determine how the mountainous public lands may best be used recreationally in all seasons. The club—the members who have made the club and who have been the club—has done much.

Much remains to be done, and the club will have to be increasingly vigilant in the future, because the western trend of population will inevitably bring new demands for destructive inroads on our park and wilderness areas—a superlative national resource of scenic beauty that men of vision set aside not only for those who came after them, but also for those who will come after us.

Muiriana

THE SIERRA CLUB is collecting for its library material by and about John Muir. It has already acquired by gift many photographs of John Muir taken at various times during his later life; the letters which he, as president of the club, wrote to William E. Colby, its secretary, over a period of nearly fifteen years; the many letters which he wrote to Vernon and Charlotte Kellogg; and the extremely important (from a conservation standpoint) letters written by Muir to Robert Underwood Johnson leading up to the creation of Yosemite National Park and concerning the recession of the Yosemite Valley State Park to the United States. The club desires to add to this collection and will appreciate any further gifts of photographs and letters, which will be carefully preserved.

A collection of slides showing background scenes of Muir's life, from his childhood in Scotland through his youth in Wisconsin to the far-ranging activities of his later years, has been prepared by Barbara Lachelt and sets are available for purchase.

The Sierra Club on the National Scene

SON OF THE WILDERNESS and father of the Sierra Club, John Muir was already nationally prominent when he became the club's first president 64 years ago. His concern for the emerging National Park system, and for the forest reserves which later became the national forests, was a concern which the club shared. That concern has never diminished.

The club's name came from California's Sierra Nevada. The early conservation program centered in the Sierra Nevada. So did most of the first wilderness outings, which John Muir and William E. Colby started in order to bring more people into intimate contact with the Range of Light as it was then, and as it could remain if enough people knew it to protect it. As the central Sierra was the focus of activity, so was central California the focus of membership. Of the 182 charter members (of whom three are still living), 175 were from the San Francisco Bay region, many of them drawn from the faculties of the University of California and Stanford University. Of the remaining seven, two were from the San Joaquin Valley, Galen Clark was the Yosemite member, there were lone members in Seattle, New York, and Utah, and in Santa Barbara—that far south!

But "sierra" means, among other things, "saw-toothed mountain range," and these exist all over the West. Growing interest in travel to scenic places brought people from all over the country to these places, and problems came with the people. A good number of the travelers joined Sierra Club trips and then stayed with the club to help solve the problems.

In two of the early conservation battles the club enlisted nation-wide support. The first was to persuade the State of California to give Yosemite Valley back to the federal government. We won. The second was to persuade the city of San Francisco not to invade Hetch Hetchy Valley, part of Yosemite National Park, for water and power development for which there were (and still are) alternatives. We lost, but gained lasting support; with Hetch Hetchy as a horrible example, the creation of an enduring National Park system could be expedited. There was enough nation-wide conservation coöperation to make the National Park Act become law in 1916. Five of the six Directors of the National Park Service have been members of the Sierra Club. Stephen T. Mather, the first Director, first became interested in the national parks on a Sierra Club High Trip.

The early battles for the parks demonstrated how important it is to fight off a threat wherever it first appears. An invasion of Yellowstone, of Glacier, of Olympic, of Jackson Hole, would serve only to strengthen the hand of those who might soon wish to exploit the parks close to the home base. The Sierra Club fought off dangers in these, at first distant, fields as soon as they arose. In the earliest fights it was joined by, or joined with, the Appalachian Mountain Club, the Prairie Club, and the organization which has since become the American Planning and Civic Association. On the West Coast it coöperated with such pioneer organizations as the Mazamas and the Mountaineers, a coöperation which finally led to the creation of the Federation of Western Outdoor Clubs. Other organizations appeared on the national scene; of these, those whose programs most nearly paralleled the Sierra Club's and with which the club worked most closely, were the National Parks Association (1919), the Izaak Walton League of America (1922), and the Wilderness Society (1935).

The national community of interest led in 1947 to the formation of the Natural Resources Council of America, in which the club soon became an active participant, its executive director becoming chairman of the Council in 1955. The Council sought the creation of a committee on conservation to advise the Secretary of the Interior. The then president of the club was named to the first committee.

The Natural Resources Council was something new. It is not an action organization seeking to impose a common will upon the 37 national organizations that belong to it. The Council is primarily a forum. It provides an occasion which did not previously exist for leaders of these organizations to meet and to share knowledge, and to continue sharing knowledge after they return to their respective headquarters.

This is the force, this new unity among conservationists, which the proponents of Echo Park dam ran head into in what became the most important battle for the national park idea since the invasion of Hetch Hetchy. The many organizations who joined to protect Dinosaur were disparate in kind. Some were technical societies, some were primarily of fishermen, others of hunters, of mountaineers, of people who especially like birds or gardens or wild places in general. Possibly the only one thing they had in common was a devotion to the abstract concept that wilderness has values which our culture cannot afford to lose, and that this is an important part of living for something besides making a living. Whatever it was they shared, they worked in concert and they won. The Sierra Club was one of the instruments that played in that concert. The combined harmony produced a magnificent symphony, and we shall need to keep the score at hand and play it again from time to time.

The Club's Conservationist Role

FOR SIXTEEN YEARS before the word *conservation* became popular, the Sierra Club was practicing it, just as John Muir had before the club was founded. *Conservation* has meant many things, and through the years members of the club have individually been interested in all of them, including the conservation of soil, water, forests, and materials in general—conservation in the sense of wise use, with minimum waste, of the resources the earth affords for man's economy. The club itself, however, has never been more than indirectly concerned with the economics of resource conservation. From the beginning its specialty has been the preservation of natural scenery, in national parks and monuments, in national-forest recreation areas, in wilderness under whatever jurisdiction, in state and local parks, together with a deep interest in the wildlife that makes these places complete. Whether justifiably or not, those who work for conservation of natural scenery and wildlife have come to be known as conservationists, a term which excludes the people who have a role in managing a resource for profit, even though they may conserve it in doing so.

Thus the Sierra Club is a group of conservationists, active and potentially active, whose interest in the cause of conservation has received its impetus from direct knowledge of scenic America which the members have acquired in the club's program of outings and other outdoor activities. This, at least, was the principal stimulus of conservation interest in the early decades of the club. More recently there has been a pronounced rise in the number who support the club solely to further its public-service program, only rarely to enjoy its activities.

In all its program, the club has carefully avoided taking action that would benefit itself or its members any more than it would benefit the public as a whole. This does not mean that the club has not been misunderstood at times. For example, it has always been easy for people who have not known the whole story to assume that because the club advocates the preservation of wilderness and also conducts wilderness outings, the club therefore strives to protect wilderness for its own selfish purposes. While it is true that the club's wilderness outings would cease if there were no wilderness, so would all wilderness outings, whatever their sponsorship—and the club's contribution to wilderness travel in toto is very minute. Moreover, the club outings are nonprofit.

The club, in its conservationist role, has placed special emphasis on wilderness preservation in the last quarter century (which saw the dropping of the words "to render accessible" from the club's purposes because

[13]

too many people thought this meant "accessible by road or tramway") because wilderness, after all, is the most precious of our scenic possessions. It is least likely to get support from the branch of conservation devoted to resource management. And it can never be replaced if the resource managers covet it successfully.

Which brings us, as conservationists, full circle—back to where we collectively need to keep our conservation interest broad enough to be aware enough of resource-management needs to preserve wilderness from management. For instance, wilderness will be safest from exploitation by lumbermen if the extensive tree-bearing areas that need not be wild are managed with maximum long-range efficiency. It behooves us, then, to know enough about the technique of forestry to know when it is not efficient—to be able to point out to the lumbermen who covet the wilderness rain forest of Olympic National Park that there are five other ways, if they operate efficiently, to get the lumber Olympic's dedicated forests could produce but should not.

Through the years the Club's Board of Directors have made a series of conservationist decisions, duly recorded in the minutes, that constitute the club's policy on park and wilderness matters. These are currently compiled in a Policy and Procedure Guide that is revised as necessary from time to time. The club depends heavily upon volunteer effort—a reservoir of freely volunteered skills, inspiration, and hard work that have made the club a major national force in its conservationist role.

The volunteer effort shows itself in many ways in the conservation program. It may be all but unsung, as it is with the thousands of members who, upon learning of a need, write letters that need to be written to men who will make decisions. Less obscure but still not heralded is the work of the committees of the club who help tell of the conservation need— the conservation committees in the chapters who study the local problems, and the chapter editorial committees and action committees who spread the understanding. In all the chapters there is opportunity to serve on these task forces—to give much time if you have it, or slightly less if you are exceedingly busy with other affairs. There are special missions for people who have retired from competing, mundane activity and have time to contribute in big chunks.

Better known, but never heralded enough, are the members of the Conservation Committee of the club as a whole, which coördinates the effort of the chapter conservation committees and which, with the help of collaborators all over the country, keeps posted on the nation's scenic-conservation needs, studies them, does conservation staff work for the Board of Directors, and acts upon behalf of the club once policy is established. Theirs are fascinating meetings, well attended, and open to all who would like to help the entire program or to concentrate upon a special project.

The club's Board of Directors meet three or four times a year and make policy decisions on conservation. The Executive Committee of the Board meets at least that often to act on behalf of the Board as needed. When the pressure is on, the Executive Committee can make decisions between meetings in a day or two. If immediate action is necessary, the Conservation Administration Committee (the President, his designee, Conservation Committee Chairman, and the Executive Director), can make decisions and act upon them in a matter of minutes.

Such a range of flexibility could be hazardous. Continuity keeps it from being so. In its whole history of volunteer effort the club has been one of the most fortunate in the country in its carry-over of knowledge. The club has not been exclusive in the sense you would expect from an organization which is a club instead of an association or society. But it has suffered not one whit by being everyman's. It has vitality enough in what it is doing to encourage an 89-year-old—as the best example—to take out a life membership after he has been paying dues for decades. That same vitality, that feeling that the club can somehow give one of participating in important accomplishment, in doing things that *do* make a difference a hundred years from now, has kindled and kept aflame a devotion that keeps the same people together, yet without excluding the new and the young. There have been just three chairmen of the Outing Committee in its 59 years of operation. This could conceivably mean stultification. It means everything else, including the most vital outing program in the club's history. Some members of the Board of Directors have served for two decades. Others are brand new, some of them ready to grow old in the service, others to make way. It all adds up to continuity, to being able to carry on one year where the club left off the last, rather than going back to the beginning to start all over. And continuity, plus the variety of professional skills freely contributed by top men, have made the Sierra Club a force you can predict, respect, count upon, and reckon with.

There is a certain limit to what volunteers can do; for the most part, they must unfortunately give priority to their means of livelihood. The club's conservation program survived this limitation, however slight, for 60 years. In 1952 the position of Executive Director was established, and there was then a member of the club whom the President could *tell* to represent it, near and far, instead of asking. Several times each year this has enabled the club to be represented in Washington when it probably could not have been otherwise. But this, the Executive Director urges, must always be a complementary effort, never a substitute for what has always given the club its exemplary strength—you, its volunteer member.

How Much for Their Signature?

Is IT PROFITABLE for the individual to build a beautiful home? To give his children a higher education? No, it is seldom profitable, yet we do both. These are, in fact, ethical and aesthetic premises which underlie the economic system. Once accepted, economic forces tend to align the smaller details of social organization into harmony with them.

No such ethical premise yet exists for the condition of the land these children must live in. Our children are our signature to the roster of history; our land is merely the place our money was made. There is as yet no social stigma in the possession of a gullied farm, a wrecked forest, or a polluted stream, provided the dividends suffice to send the youngsters to college. Whatever ails the land, the government will fix it.

I think we have here the root of the problem. What conservation education must build is an ethical underpinning for land economics and a universal curiosity to understand the land mechanism. Conservation may then follow.

—ALDO LEOPOLD, in *Round River* (Oxford, 1953)

Sierra or Sierras?

THE SPANISH word *sierra* means "range of mountains," and is usually found in combination with other words, such as Sierra Blanca (White Range), Sierra Madre (Mother Range, or Central Range), and Sierra Nevada (Snowy Range). Occasionally *las sierras* is used to designate a group of mountain ranges or ridges. In the Spanish narratives of exploration *una sierra nevada* is frequently found written without capital initials, referring simply to a snow-covered range of mountains. It was in this way that our own Sierra Nevada was first designated. Early in the nineteenth century it was sometimes called the California Range by American explorers, but gradually the Spanish phrase prevailed, and after a while it became a specific name and took its place on all maps. The Sierra Nevada is distinctly a unit, both geographically and topographically, and is well described as *"una sierra nevada."* Strictly speaking, therefore, we should never say "Sierras," or "High Sierras," or "Sierra Nevadas," in referring to it. Nevertheless, these forms are so frequently found in the very best works of literature and science that it would perhaps be pedantic to deny their admissibility. It becomes, therefore, a matter of preference, and for our part we rather like to keep in mind the unity of our great range by calling it simply "The Sierra" or "The Sierra Nevada."

Having thus promised not to look askance at "Sierras," we may perhaps be spared the pain of hearing "Sierra Nevada Mountains." Surely one does not say "Loch Katrine Lake," "Rio Grande River," or "Saint San Francisco."

HOLOGRAPH

I HAVE congenital hunting fever and three sons. As little tots, they spent their time playing with my decoys and scouring vacant lots with wooden guns. I hope to leave them good health, an education, and possibly even a competence. But what are they going to do with these things if there is no more deer in the hills, and no more quail in the coverts? No more snipe whistling in the meadow, no more piping of widgeons and chattering of teal as darkness covers the marshes; no more whistling of swift wings when the morning star pales in the east? And when the dawnwind stirs through the ancient cottonwoods, and the gray light steals down from the hills over the old river sliding softly past its wide brown sandbars— what if there be no more goose music?

—ALDO LEOPOLD, in *Round River* (Oxford, 1953)

Publications

WRITING and publishing have always been important activities of the Sierra Club. While the complete list of publications is a varied one, most of the club's publishing energy has been concentrated on the *Sierra Club Bulletin,* published without interruption since 1893 and recognized as one of the best outdoor periodicals in the world. It has always been more serious than most mountaineering journals. Historical, scientific, and even philosophic articles make up a large part of the content. Added to these are accounts of climbing and mountain exploration in the Sierra Nevada and other western regions, conservation articles, discussions of climbing technique, notes on trips and club activities, and book reviews, so that the *Bulletin* is an extraordinarily varied and rewarding journal not only for club members but for all those interested, in one way or another, in the mountain regions of western America. Photographic illustrations by Joseph N. LeConte, Walter L. Huber, Ansel Adams, Cedric Wright, Philip Hyde, and others, have been outstanding.

The *Bulletin* is now issued monthly except July and August. One number each year is in the form of a magazine, containing the longer articles and many pages of photographic illustrations. The other issues are devoted to club announcements, to outdoor and conservation news, and particularly to the never-ending fight to defend parks, mountains, forests, lakes, and other wilderness areas against damage or exploitation by selfish groups.

The *Bulletin* and other publications are the responsibility of the club's Editorial Board, whose chairman edits the annual magazine number of the *Bulletin* and appoints the editor of the monthly issues. Staff members assist the editors, but contributions are welcomed from all sources. Any club member who has an article, a picture, a drawing, a suggestion, or a criticism to offer should get in touch with the appropriate editor.

A list of the back numbers of the *Bulletin* that are still available is maintained at the club office. The earliest numbers have long since been out of print, but recently, through the offset process, they have been made available in five bound volumes. Other out-of-print numbers will be reissued from time to time by the same process. A *Fifty-seven-Year Index* (1893–1949) was published in 1952.

WRITERS AND EDITORS

High standards have been set for the *Bulletin,* both in content and in editorial work, by the many professional scholars, writers, and editors who have been members of the club. On occasion, distinguished writers not connected with the club have cheerfully made contributions of substantial value. In the earlier days the Editorial Board was composed largely of university men, especially from the University of California and from Stanford.

Professor J. Henry Senger, of California, headed the first Committee on Publications, 1893–1894. Cornelius Beach Bradley, Professor of English in the University of California, was editor from 1895 to 1897. He was succeeded by Warren Gregory, who was in charge for the next two years. From 1900 to 1903 David Starr Jordan, then president of Stanford University, was chairman of the Committee on Publications and James S. Hutchinson, San Francisco attorney, was assistant editor. Hutchinson became editor later in 1903. Elliott McAllister succeeded him in 1905 and held the position through 1910. He in turn was succeeded by Dr. William Frederic Badè, noted authority on Old Testament literature and archaeological exploration and later editor of the *Life and Letters of John Muir.* Dr. Badè was editor from 1911 to 1922, C. Nelson Hackett from 1923 to 1924, and James S. Hutchinson again in 1925. Francis P. Farquhar, having already served twelve years on the Editorial Board, took charge in 1926 and edited the *Bulletin* for twenty years. It was under him that the *Bulletin* reached its present high standard and became known as the best of its kind editorially and typographically. Among the best known contributions in this period have been Mr. Farquhar's own studies of the human history and exploration of the Sierra Nevada. An appreciation of his work is to be found in the 1946 annual number, page 112. David R. Brower, author of many mountaineering articles and editor of the *Manual of Ski Mountaineering, Going Light with Backpack or Burro,* and other publications, was editor from 1946 until he became the first Executive Director of the club in 1953. The present chairman of the Editorial Board, August Frugé, the director of the University of California Press, has edited the annual magazine numbers since 1953, while a separate staff has edited the regular monthly issues.

Books

In 1900 Joseph LeConte's *A Journal of Ramblings Through the High Sierra by the University Excursion Party,* first published privately in 1875, was republished in the *Bulletin* and printed separately as a book. This edition subsequently became nearly as scarce as the first one, and in 1930 the club published a new edition with a foreword by Francis P. Farquhar. The *Journal* records the experiences and impressions of Professor LeConte on a trip to the Yosemite region on horseback in the summer of 1870 and is one of the classics of High Sierra literature.

Place Names of the High Sierra, by Francis P. Farquhar, was published in three installments in the *Bulletins* of 1923, 1924 and 1925, and then reissued as a separate book in 1926. The book is now out of print; a revised edition is in preparation.

The *Guide to the John Muir Trail and the High Sierra Region*, by Walter A. Starr, Jr., was first published in 1934, and has been revised and reprinted several times. This detailed guide to the trails of the High Sierra from the Tuolumne to the Kern and the Kaweah, with descriptions of approaches and laterals from the east and west, was begun by Walter A. Starr, Jr. After "Pete" Starr's accidental death in The Minarets, the book was completed by his father, Walter A. Starr.

Beginning in 1937, climbing guides to various regions in the Sierra were published in the *Bulletin*, with the expectation that when all regions had been covered and corrections had been made, a comprehensive guide would be published. A preliminary edition embodying all parts published serially in the *Bulletin* was issued in 1949, and in 1954 the first edition of *A Climber's Guide to the High Sierra* was published, under the editorship of Hervey Voge—and reprinted in 1956.

Shortly before the United States entered World War II, a group of Sierra Club ski mountaineers prepared, under the auspices of the National Ski Association, the *Manual of Ski Mountaineering*, a book on the technique of travel, camping, and climbing in the mountains of western America. This book, which has a military as well as a recreational value, was published in 1942 by the University of California Press. The second edition, issued in 1946 and reprinted in 1947, was revised and expanded from experience gained during the war on mountains all over the world. The club became publisher in 1960.

A similar manual for backpackers and for others who wish to travel the mountains without horses, mules, jeeps, or helicopters, was published in 1951, and has been reprinted four times: *Going Light—With Backpack or Burro*.

A Climber's Guide to the Teton Range and *Belaying the Leader: An Omnibus on Climbing Safety*, appeared in 1956, marking further expansion of the club's interest in safety and mountaineering beyond the Sierra Nevada.

In 1950 John Muir's articles on the geology of the Sierra Nevada, published originally in the *Overland Monthly* and reprinted in various early numbers of the *Bulletin*, were collected and published in a separate volume entitled *John Muir's Studies in the Sierra,* with a detailed introduction by William E. Colby.

As the great Dinosaur controversy neared its close, the club realized the importance of a book on the area. The Executive Director outlined the book, assembled the illustrations, the contributors (all but one were members), the editor, and the publisher; *This Is Dinosaur: Echo Park Country and Its Magic Rivers,* edited by Wallace Stegner, was published by Alfred Knopf early in 1955. The club also had much to do with the promotion and distribution of the book.

The publishing program entered a new era in 1960 with publication of the club's first major work, *This Is the American Earth,* by Ansel Adams and Nancy Newhall. This brought a new dimension to club publishing and led to the Board's authorizing that a full-time editor and publications manager be engaged.

CHAPTER PUBLICATIONS

Monthly, semimonthly, and irregular news sheets are issued by several groups. First of these to appear was *Mugelnoos,* written and distributed every month by the Ski Mountaineers Section of the Angeles Chapter.

Next to appear, and the first chapter newspaper, was *The Yodeler,* established by the San Francisco Bay Chapter in 1939.

Other chapter publications are similar to *The Yodeler.* The *Southern Sierran,* published by the Angeles Chapter, was begun in 1946. It is published monthly.

The Bonanza, a mimeographed news sheet of several pages, is published in Sacramento by the Mother Lode Chapter. *Hi Sierrans* is issued by the San Diego Chapter; *Palm and Pine* by the Riverside Chapter; *The Loma Prietan* by the Loma Prieta Chapter; *The Argonaut* by the Atlantic Chapter; *The Kern-Kaweah Newsletter* by the Kern-Kaweah Chapter; *The Condor Call* by the Los Padres Chapter; *Tehipite Topics* by the Tehipite Chapter, and the Pacific Northwest Chapter *Newsletter* and Great Lakes Chapter *Newsletter.*

All chapters issue, from time to time, schedules of forthcoming walks, educational events, climbs, parties, entertainment, and other activities.

What Can a Mountain Mean?

As the years have passed, the trend of exploration has become more sharply focused on the intimate aspects of the scene; rock climbing, skiing, creative pictorial and literary expression have taken the place of the pilgrimages of the earlier years. Our exploration today is as vital and as urgent a program as it ever was. We are, however, transcribing exploration into experience; we are seeking a closer contact and deeper understanding of the natural scene in both its vast and delicate aspects. Our ultimate function was never the mere making of maps and the collation of physical data; rather it was to interpret the assembled facts in terms of enjoyment and spiritual experience, and to assist others to seek and comprehend the heart of nature.

After all, in the strictly materialistic sense, a mountain is simply an object of inanimate stone garnished with vegetation. It can be measured, weighed, climbed, and even removed or destroyed. Gravity, weather, geologic processes determine its form and the flow of the rivers at its base. These streams possess potential water power, provide irrigation, and contain fish. The timber on the slopes may be salable, and on the surface and inside of the mountain valuable minerals may be found and mined.

Obviously, the *corpus* and the spirit of the mountain are two very different entities. A mountain provides an impressive symbol of the wonder and beauty of the natural world, of contact with the primal purities of nature, of the cleanliness and the emotional stimulus of the realities of the earth.

IE WORLD OF STONE AND SPACE AND SKY . . .

PHOTOGRAPHS AND TEXT BY ANSEL ADAMS

. . . OF SIMPLE GROWING THINGS . . .

. . OF THE ANTIQUITIES OF MAN . . .

. . . AND THE ANTIQUITIES OF NATURE . . .

. REVEALS TO ALL PEOPLE . . .

. . . THE PATTERNS OF ETERNITY.

E WHO HAS KNOWN THE JUBILANCE OF MORNINGS . . .

. . . AND THE QUIETNESS OF DUSK . . .

. . THE FLASH OF WATERS IN THE SUN . . .

. . . THE SOLEMNITY OF STORM . . .

. THE VIGOR OF THE SKY . . .

. . . AND THE ENDURANCE OF THE ARID LANDS

ATTENDS THE RITUALS OF SPRING . . .

. . . THE LIVING FIRES OF AUTUMN

. THE QUIETNESS OF WINTER . . .

AND BECOMES ONE WITH THE WORLD.

Mountaineering

THERE HAVE always been a good many people in the Sierra Club whose enjoyment of the mountains seems to vary with the altitude, reaching its climax when they have made their way to a high and rugged peak. Why they should enjoy climbing no nonclimber has ever quite been able to understand, possibly because no climber has yet been able to make his reasons quite clear, in all the hundreds of thousands of pages of mountaineering literature. John Muir exhorted people to go to the mountains to get their glad tidings. Some go for adventure. Others have gone for exercise, for science, for sport, for romance, for meeting a challenge, for measuring themselves. The fact remains that people climb mountains, and that there were many mountaineers among the organizers of the club. Mountaineering has been one of the club's chief interests ever since.

The members who climbed in the early days were men who found their way into the mountains independently, explored and learned about the California heights and those farther afield, and wanted others to experience the same joys. Many peaks familiar to us, which have been climbed so often now, were then almost unknown. It is hard to realize that well-trodden Mount Ritter, although first climbed by John Muir in 1872, was not visited again for eleven years, when Willard Johnson and John Miller, of the U. S. Geological survey, reached the summit. Nine years went by before Joseph N. LeConte, Hubert Dyer, Theodore Solomons, and Sidney Peixotto made another ascent—in 1892, the year of the Sierra Club's birth. Solomons explored and climbed at the head of the San Joaquin in 1894 and 1895.

In 1893 the Sierra Club published two maps of the Sierra prepared by Joseph N. LeConte which were amplified and consolidated in a single sheet in 1896. These did much to encourage members to explore and report on the less well-known parts of the high country. In the summer of 1896 a remarkable amount of pioneer work was done. Professor Bolton Coit Brown covered the area from Mount Clarence King, over the Kings-Kern Divide, to Mount Williamson, and made the first ascent of Clarence King. His sketches of the country and the peaks were of great help to later mountaineers. Walter A. Starr and Allan L. Chickering, accompanied part way by Solomons, left Yosemite in early July of that same year, and explored the upper Merced and beyond. Their object was to photograph and map the connecting strip of the crest between Yosemite and the Kings River Canyon. They came back with valuable topographic data and photographs. LeConte, with a party of four, packed into the Bubbs Creek region, accompanied Brown on the first ascent of Mount Gardiner, and with the rest of his party climbed University Peak and Mount Brewer.

Much remarkable exploration was achieved by Sierra Club members in those early days, when many of our familiar trails did not exist. An outstanding trip was that of Joseph N. LeConte, Duncan McDuffie, and James S. Hutchinson, who in the summer of 1908 traveled south from Tuolumne, made the first ascent of Mount Abbot, continued on through the Evolution basin, over Muir Pass, down LeConte Canyon to the middle fork of Kings River, and eventually reached Kanawyer's Camp. There was no trail, and they had to find a way for the mules to go. They traveled 228 miles over this high mountain route (with side trips, about 300 miles) in 27 days.

It was this sort of pioneering by our predecessors that helped to give us our present-day easy routes to the high country and to the peaks. What they learned of timberline and of canyon, of mountaineering in many phases, has been handed down to later generations of the club.

Outing Climbs, and the Coming of the Rope

When the first High Trip was conducted, the chance came for more than a hardy few to climb those distant, inaccessible mountains. Many who never would have been able to become acquainted with the high peaks or even to imagine setting foot upon them, now found it possible.

On the first Outing, in 1901, at Tuolumne Meadows, fairly large groups were led by experienced men up Mount Hoffmann and Mount Dana. William E. Colby led twenty up Mount Lyell, probably the largest group to have climbed it up to that time. On the Outing in 1902, only those with a mountaineering record of high climbing were allowed to attempt Mount Brewer (and because of the hazards, no skirts were to be worn by the ladies). The next year Mount Williamson was climbed by a large party, including the first women to make the ascent. The *San Francisco Chronicle* of September 6 of that year headed an article by Edward T. Parsons about the climb, "First Women to Scale Mount Williamson . . . Members of Sierra Club Achieve that Honor . . . Most Difficult Peak of the Sierras." In 1903 also, Joseph N. LeConte made the first ascent of North Palisade with James K. Moffitt and James S. Hutchinson.

Mount Whitney of course has been the goal of many Sierra Club expeditions as well as of individuals. In 1902, after the Outing in Kings Canyon, a party was organized to return to the region in order to climb Mount

Whitney. John Muir was the leader of that "galaxy of stars," which included Theodore H. Hittell, seventy-two years old; C. Hart Merriam, of the Biological Survey; Henry Gannett, of the U. S. Geological Survey; William Keith, the painter; Marion Hooker, grand-niece of Professor Josiah Whitney, for whom the mountain was named; and several others. (See the Story of Mount Whitney, *SCB*, May, 1947.) The next year, 1903, began the series of ascents by large groups from the Outing. Joseph N. LeConte led the first group of about forty to the top; a few days later, William E. Colby led the main party, numbering in all one hundred and three. Now, more than forty years later, accessible though it is, there is still a thrill for many when they reach the highest point in the United States. Nothing has changed the magnificence of the view.

It was not only the California mountains that lured the early Sierrans. A notable achievement was the trip to Mount Rainier in 1905, instigated by Edward T. Parsons. A party was selected from qualified mountaineers, and divided into companies of ten, each in charge of an experienced captain. Fifty-six persons, including fifteen women, made the ascent from Camp Muir in five hours. There were sixty-one persons on the summit of Rainier that day, July 25—the largest recorded party to make the climb in any one day.

And so through the years mountaineering lessons learned through the club have made it possible for many to climb independently and safely our own mountains and other mountains all over the world—and most important of all, to pass down the knowledge to the new members who, until guided by the Sierra Club, have had no chance to learn the fine and rewarding art of climbing.

Outstanding among members who have helped others gain mountain experience is Norman Clyde, whose amazing achievements in scaling practically all the peaks in the High Sierra are well known to mountaineers. More than one climber has exulted in a supposedly first ascent, only to find later that Clyde went up that "unclimbed" peak in the winter of, say, 1920! There are many seasoned climbers who can look back on their early days as novices in the mountains and remember with gratitude what they learned from Clyde. In the course of many High Trips, he has led hundreds of members up peaks. Almost all Sierrans who have developed the passion for climbing acquired that passion from some other member, if not from Norman Clyde, who gave them a boost by sharing his enthusiasm and his knowledge of how to do it.

In 1931, while the High Trip was exploring the Yosemite High Sierra, a decided step forward in mountain climbing was made. Through the efforts of Francis P. Farquhar and Robert L. M. Underhill, the latter of the Appalachian Mountain Club, the proper use of the rope was introduced to a number of persons on the outing. Although some members had previously used ropes on more difficult peaks, there had not been much serious consideration of perfecting rope technique and making it understood by all. Thus, the year 1931 marked the beginning of the development in the club of the art of climbing with ropes.

The next year a small enthusiastic group, inspired by Richard M. Leonard and calling itself the Cragmont Climbing Club, began practicing on local rocks, chiefly on Cragmont Rock in Berkeley. From this group developed the Rock Climbing Section of the San Francisco Bay Chapter. Subsequently, climbing sections were organized in several other chapters.

These sections exist primarily to give members the opportunity to learn safe climbing methods on near-by rocks, so that they may then climb in the high mountains with safety and assurance. On Sierra Club climbs one of the important requirements is that all participants practice belaying. Climbers learn to check practice falls, smoothly and effectively.

The more thoughtful and also, perhaps, the more ingenious climbers in the club have tried to improve on known methods in order to make safety a positive factor in climbing and not just a desirable possibility. Leonard contributed greatly to the advancement of mountaineering safety by initiating the dynamic belay. This is the technique of checking a high fall by easing it to a stop—by letting the climbing rope *slide* around the belayer's hips and over the belay point so that the kinetic energy of a high fall can be checked by a force that is small enough for both belayer and climber to withstand. This was a marked advance over the fixed belay practiced earlier—and still—in Europe. (See *Belaying the Leader: An Omnibus on Climbing Safety*, 1956.)

Of course, the most important part of rock-climbing instruction was —and is—instruction in how not to fall. Beginners receive their first lessons either very close to the ground or protected by a belay from above in order that they may make mistakes—many of them—and fall often without harm to themselves. In this way they can safely climb up to the limit of their ability, even beyond that limit, and thus find out precisely where that limit is. They will then be able, when out in the mountains and lacking the safeguards of practice climbs, to keep a respectful distance short of that limit. Practice climbs teach the climber how to measure his margin of safety and maintain it. The technique of the rope—of knots and belays—when properly learned, will provide the additional factor of safety needed should the climber miscalculate his margin. For the more severe climbs, pitons or expansion bolts may be needed for safety. Sierra Club members have led the way in the application of these aids in many difficult ascents in America and elsewhere.

Climbing technique and equipment devised by Sierra Club mountaineers won national recognition in the course of World War II through the work of mountaineers in the Office of the Quartermaster General, in which Richard M. Leonard, Einar Nilsson, Bestor Robinson, and Phil von Lubken worked in the Special Forces Section; and in the army's mountain training program, in which an important contribution to climbing instruction for six infantry divisions was made by Artur Argiewicz, Jr., Raffi Bedayn, David R. Brower, Chester L. Errett, Charles W. Hanks, Milton Hildebrand, Solon R. Lindsey, Rolf Pundt, and Jack Riegelhuth. Much of the doctrine in the army manual, *Mountain Operations (FM 70–10)* had its beginnings on Cragmont Rock.

Major Ascents

Alaskan peaks early beckoned to Sierra Club climbers. In 1892 Mark B. Kerr made an attempt to reach the summit of Mount St. Elias but was unsuccessful (*SCB*, January, 1893). Fifty years after the first ascent in 1897 by the Duke of Abruzzi (*SCB*, 1898) the *Bulletin* carried the account by Dee Molenaar, a member of the club, of the second ascent (and first American ascent) of the mountain, accomplished by a small party in the summer of 1946.

Highest of all North American mountains, Mount McKinley (20,300) has always been the dream of Western climbers. Sierra Club members have felt a link with all explorations on the mountain, if only through their interest in them, but it was in 1942 that the club felt really a part of the expedition on the mountain that year. A group testing equipment for the army used Mount McKinley for its trial grounds, and incidentally attained both summits. Einar Nilsson was a member of the group reaching the top. In 1953, Fritz Lippmann climbed McKinley with another group.

Among notable climbs by club members or club groups have been:

The first ascent of the Cathedral Spires in Yosemite in 1934, by Jules Eichorn, Richard Leonard, and Bestor Robinson. This was the first use of pitons in the Sierra Nevada.

Two attempts on Mount Waddington (Mystery Mountain) in Canada, in 1935 and 1936, and an attempt on Kate's Needle, Alaska, in 1937.

The successful ascent of Shiprock, outstanding peak of northwestern New Mexico, in October, 1939, by Raffi Bedayn, David R. Brower, John A. Dyer, and Bestor Robinson.

The climb of Snowpatch Spire in the Bugaboos of the Purcell Range, in 1940, by Raffi Bedayn and Jack Arnold.

The first ascent of the "unclimbable" Lost Arrow in Yosemite Valley, by Jack Arnold, Robin Hansen, Fritz Lippmann, and Anton Nelson, who climbed from the Valley rim in 1946. Nelson and John Salathé made the ascent from the bottom a year later.

The first ascent, also in 1947, by Ruth and John Mendenhall, of the oft-tried Mount Confederation, in Canada.

A third expedition to the Waddington country by a Sierra Club group, in 1947, on which many first ascents were made.

Still another expedition to the Waddington region of British Columbia in 1950, during which many ascents were accomplished, including two new routes up Mount Waddington.

In recent years many extremely difficult rock climbs have been completed in the Sierra. In 1950 Castle Rock Spire, in Sequoia National Park, was first ascended by Philip C. Bettler, William Long, Will Siri, Allen Steck, and James Wilson. The same year the complete ascent of the north face of Sentinel Rock, in Yosemite, was made by John Salathé and Steck, in a tour de force requiring four bivouacs. In 1952 Steck and Robert Swift climbed the Yosemite Point Buttress. The same year the famous tree on the face of El Capitan was reached by William Dunmire, Will Siri, Steck, and Swift. A noteworthy climb in 1953 was that of the east buttress of El Capitan in three days by William Long, Willi Unsoeld, Siri, and Steck.

Club members have lately been roaming still farther afield in the search for new mountains to conquer, and new experiences in mountain wildernesses. Individuals or groups have climbed in the Alps, Mexico, Canada, Alaska, South America, and Nepal. In 1950 Will Siri accompanied a scientific expedition to Peru and climbed Yanasinga. In 1951 Alfred W. Baxter, Jr., Rupert Gates, and Jon Lindbergh went to the Saint Elias Range and made first ascents of Mount Bear and Mount Jordan.

The Cordillera Blanca of Peru beckoned as a range of outstanding peaks, with more than 29 summits exceeding 20,000 feet. When a Sierra Club group went there in 1952, the first ascent of the east peak of Huandoy was completed by Allen Steck, Will Siri, Fletcher Hoyt, and Peter Hoessly. Nevado Pisco was also climbed. In 1954 Richard Irvin was a member of an American party which made many ascents in the Cordillera Blanca. Leigh Ortenburger, author of the club's Teton guide, contributed many beautiful photographs of the region to the *Bulletin.*

The California Himalayan Expedition in 1954 was the most ambitious undertaking yet launched by club climbers. The goal was Makalu (27,790) in Nepal, world's fourth [or fifth] highest peak. The party consisted of William Dunmire, Richard Houston, Fritz Lippmann, William Long, Bruce Meyer, Nello Pace, Will Siri, Al Steck, Larry Swan, and Willi Unsoeld. They found a way to the mountain through almost unknown territory, reconnoitered two alternative routes, and set up a series of five camps on the southeast ridge route, with Camp III at the south col. Because of bad weather they had to turn back at 23,700 feet. The venture was initially conceived of by Alfred Baxter, but he was unable to go himself. The club provided an advisory committee and helped raise and disburse the funds. A small residual expedition fund resulted.

While the Makalu expedition was the first to the Himalaya on which all expedition members were club members too, club-trained mountaineers were present on several others, outstanding among which was the ascent of Hidden Peak by an expedition organized and ably led by club member Nick Clinch.

At this writing it can be predicted fairly safely that there will be more expeditions and that the Himalaya will become better known, thanks in small part to club members, not only in its geography—but possibly even in its recreational value. At a meeting of the Board of Directors in 1959 it was jokingly suggested, in view of the rapid growth of the club, that there might one day be a base camp on the Baltoro Glacier. Something of the kind is probably within the club's ken—and on a small scale already accomplished in outings conducted to the St. Elias region in 1956, to the Cordillera Blanca in 1958, and planned for Ruwenzori in 1960, all three organized by Alfred Baxter.

The great mountaineer, Mummery, long ago classified mountains according to increasing vulnerability. A given peak was: impossible; the most difficult climb in the Alps; an easy day for a lady. Other ranges would seem to be running the Alpine course. The literature of mountaineering could be expected to reflect this change, and it seems to be doing so, now having gone all the way from the understated climb of a real giant to the overstated conquest of a Rum Doodle, that composite of mountain melodramas. Certainly some change was reflected in the pages of the club's *Bulletin,* to which articles on various important ascents once came automatically, but more recently have failed to come even after importuning. What was once called by British author Ronald Clark "that model of all mountain periodicals" may have to trade in its old laurel!

The 1960 revision of the Handbook cannot close its mountaineering chapter without including an accolade for one of the most extraordinary of all mountaineering achievements, one not written about for the *Bulletin*. The editor once heard himself telling a lay audience that, spectacular though rock climbing had become, El Capitan had a face no rock climber would ever consider trifling with. It was climbed.

From the *American Alpine Journal* (edited by Honorary Vice President Francis Farquhar) we derive these statistics and record them here because some Sierra Club members were party to the climb and because Yosemite, with all its wonderful climbs, is practically where the club started: "The ascent took 45 days, spread over a period of 18 months. Although the face is 2900 feet high, so much altitude was lost owing to numerous pendulum traverses that a total of 3400 feet of climbing was necessary. About 675 pitons and 125 expansion bolts were used, 90 per cent of which were for direct aid. The mileage of prusiking and rappeling has not been calculated."

There are some who would wish a cannonade, not an accolade, upon the several climbers who finally achieved this ascent, possibly because each succeeding generation of climbers is not quite happy about the motives and methods of those who follow—and generations follow fast in mountaineering. The British didn't like pitons at all and spoke of the golden age of mountaineering when only bootnail and ice ax scored the mountain. The pitons-for-safety men didn't like the pitons-for-direct-aid men, who in turn, were not happy about expansion bolters. Now the bolts-for-anchors-only men aren't too sure about the bolts-for-ladders men.

Perhaps the whole problem would not have arisen if the early-day pioneers of all kinds had not been so anxious to put a cairn on everything and had thus, by their own restraint, left a little easy frontier for today's mountaineer to explore—instead of backing him into such a tight corner of vertical wilderness, with so many nasty overhangs looming there!

Wilderness Outings

Today's Sierra Club Outings are surprisingly like the first High Trip into the Yosemite country, when the century was new. There have been several new kinds of trip; new methods, equipment and clothing; and different people. The routes and the modes of travel by which the mountains are now approached, the new trails leading to the farthest uplands, and the towns and power dams where once were meadows, all dim the memory of earlier days when the wilderness was more than a dwindling sample. But unaltered in spite of change, the purpose of any outing today—just as it was when Will Colby greeted the first Sierra Club campers at Tuolumne Meadows in 1901—is to acquaint people with the mountains. And an early High Trip accounts—for example, the one by Marion Randall in the 1905 *Bulletin*—still speaks today's language.

Merely seeing a painting of a rugged Sierra canyon or a photograph of a delicate alpine meadow cupped between granite cliffs, reading about the whispering of a forest stirred by night breezes, or having someone tell you of the grandeur of a white, pounding waterfall, can never be a substitute—no matter how skilled the artist or narrator—for experiencing mountain days and nights for yourself. You who have known the fragrance of an albicaulis bedsite, who have wondered that exhilaration and humility can be so strangely mingled as you stand upon a magnificent peak, who have mused, quiet and alone, where a stream runs through a sun-dappled grove—you are sure to oppose the violation of meadow or forest or stream more vigorously if you have felt their spell.

Knowing, then, that the person who actually visited the high places would be most concerned about their protection, John Muir and his associates built a Sierra Club devoted to the preservation of mountain wilderness. Nine years after the cornerstone was laid, the Annual Outings were inaugurated.

Beginning with that first outing in 1901, Sierra Club High Trips—and, more recently, the several variations on the original theme—have visited and revisited every part of the High Sierra from Mount Whitney to Yosemite, as well as various Western wonderlands. It would be hard even to guess how many people have thus been introduced to the mountain world, but summer after summer oldtimers have watched the metamorphosis from freshman to mountaineer, and have known that the wilderness was gaining new friends.

In its earliest form, the Annual Outing—the traditional High Trip—was a base camp, from which side excursions were made for the purpose of exploring little-known country or climbing a prominent peak. The main camp might be as much as three long days from the end of the road. The side excursions usually were made with pack trains, although there were backpacking expeditions, as well. A climbing party, which often traveled several days away from the camp, might number forty or fifty, but was made up only of those who had qualified through good climbing records or by performing creditably on preliminary excursions.

Within a few years, the trips took on the aspect of those we know today. First the main camp was moved once or twice in the course of the outing; then it was moved at more frequent intervals, until the outing became the large-scale roving pack trip, unique among all mountaineering organizations, and possible only in large wilderness areas.

For half a century, then, the Annual Outing—held each year except 1918 and 1942–45, inclusive—has enabled large numbers of people to visit the mountains at small expense and (far more important!) with the minimum depletion of grazing resources. In the light of midcentury problems—never dreamed of forty years ago—the consideration of grazing is of great importance. Wilderness boundaries are shrinking and the popularity of mountain trips is growing so rapidly that we are approaching (some think we have already reached) the point at which mountain meadows simply can't support all the people who want to visit them. The High Trip fills a real need, getting the maximum number of campers into the mountains with the minimum number of pack animals—about three people per animal, as against the usual two to five head per person in small but "luxurious" private parties.

By the latter thirties the High Trip had grown so large that inauguration of additional trips of other types met with enthusiastic response. Burro trips, knapsack trips, base camps and river trips were added to the ventures sponsored by the Outing Committee. Each has its peculiar advantages, and each serves the same fundamental purpose.

ORIENTATION

The Sierra Club member about to embark on his first mountain outing may need a bit of psychological preparation. Of course, well-intentioned "old hands" may try to provide it—and he may believe either too much or too little of what they tell him.

The truth is that he must be ready to assume his share of joint responsibility, which is in inverse proportion to the cost of the trip. The camper who can cheerfully and competently cut wood, haul water, or help with cooking or pit-digging or fire-quenching, can be sure of grateful recognition. If, in addition, he can contribute to campfire programs—anything from more or less serious discourses on the natural history of the region to music or stunts—popularity awaits him. There is, however, a further requirement, more subtle but more important. It is the obligation of the individual to the group; he must be willing to seek the proper balance between self-reliance and excessive independence. Above all, he must not become a public charge: if his feet are tender, they should be taped; if he is subject to vertigo, he should keep off cliffs and talus piles; if he hasn't a good sense of direction, he should choose companions who have. Add a philosophical acceptance of the unexpected, and you have the essence of a successful and happy high tripper—or knapsacker or burro chaser or base camper or river runner.

The physical qualifications for any of the trips are more easily stated. Since the outings are at high altitudes and fairly strenuous, all persons must be in sound health; *a physical examination is strongly urged.* Those intending to go into the mountains should take some local walks and climbs to get into condition beforehand. Shoes that are to be worn in the mountains should be used and checked on these preparatory trips.

Outings are open to members of the Sierra Club, applicants for membership, or members of similar clubs; nonmembers may go if they pay an additional fee. The outings are coöperative, and each participant shares the responsibilities, in cost and in duties, as well as the pleasures.

The Knapsack Trips

How much can you take into the mountains on your back—and still have fun? Is twenty or twenty-five pounds too much? If so, the Knapsack Trips are not for you. But if you can handle that light a load, then the cache-and-carry, small-pack type of trip will take you into the out-of-the-way mountain amphitheaters and lake basins that are reserved for those who need neither trails nor packstock.

From a roadhead, the knapsackers carry a minimum of equipment and personal items as they travel to the first food cache, which has been previously laid by packstock near a select campsite. The party bases here, exploring the near-by region until the cache becomes light enough to carry easily to the next cache—perhaps by a cross-country route. In this way no more than a few meals need be carried at one time. Further saving in weight results from using light equipment and avoiding unnecessary items. The details of running camp are few, and these are shared by all in the party. The party also shares the load of the items of community equipment—at least ten pounds per person—that are taken. The moves with pack, however light, are few. Most of the days are spent in short trips from the few campsites used. The trips need not be arduous, nor need they be too easy. There are always plenty of peaks, streams, and lakes to be explored by those with energy to burn.

Qualifications are the same as those listed for the Burro Trips; the packs, however, will not be so large as to require that members learn the diamond hitch.

THE BURRO TRIPS

A Burro Trip is the outing for those who prefer not to carry even the moderate loads required of the knapsacker, who are not sedentary enough to fancy the Base Camp, and who like to rough it a little more than the high tripper. It is the outing for those who want to learn to do it on their own. Two weeks of instruction in burro management will prepare you to conduct your own trip with friends or family next season. The others in the party will be forced to eat your cooking or starve, and you will find that their cooking is better than you expect. Everybody helps make and break camp, and nobody minds at all.

From the roadhead camp a Burro Trip can follow any one of several suitable itineraries suggested by the leader. Burros require their packers to follow trails, but free them of the necessity of seeking food caches on a schedule dictated by hunger. Both route and timetable are flexible. There can be several layover days at favorite camps, and those who wish can climb peaks while others fish or loaf in the sun.

The parties are limited to twenty persons each, selected from the applicants by the Burro Trips Committee with an eye to a reasonable balance of ages and sexes. Individuals wishing to go on more than one trip will be accommodated after the deadline date if places are available. The only qualifications are good physical condition, a good disposition, a willingness to work, and a desire to learn the tricks of mountaineering and packing.

THE FAMILY BURRO TRIP

To enable parents and their children to enjoy the mountains together and to learn how to plan trips for the enjoyment of all members of the family, burro trips for families are conducted by experienced couples accompanied by their own children. The trip is planned for four families. Each has two or three burros, brings its own food and equipment, packs its own animals, and cooks as a family unit. Camping as a family unit and cooking together, the family group is not broken; yet the fellowship of other families leads to lightening the load, increasing the entertainment, aiding the instruction, and sharing the problems.

Although children of any age can be taken into the wilderness, it has been found that about four or five years of age is the earliest that children should ordinarily be brought on these trips. More depends on the child's ability than on his age. When he is able to walk five or six miles without too much prompting, take care of his necessities by himself, enjoy camp cookery and the manner of its serving, and sleep in a sleeping bag without distress, he probably is ready for such an outing.

Most of the trips are planned to move about every second day for five or six miles, with campsites on lakes or streams where there are interesting features which children enjoy. Experience has shown that the children can take such a trip often better than their seniors.

Wilderness Threshold Trip

Families are packed into some chosen area five or six miles from the roadhead, well within walking or carrying distance for the children. In this way children of all ages can participate in a wilderness experience. There is a central commissary for the ten families coöperating in each trip, and the chores are performed by the families in rotation. Most of the days are free for exploring the trails and lakes, or taking it easy in camp. Coöperative sharing of duties frees the adults for days out of camp.

The High Trip

The Annual Outing is arranged to take participants by relatively easy moves to a series of camps near the timberline country. Because of the large number of pack animals, the number of suitable campsites is somewhat limited, and the itinerary is less flexible than that of a Burro Trip. Of course, that does not mean that, once determined, the itinerary is rigidly adhered to—the management would scarcely know what to do with itself if it were not devising a new schedule at least every other day throughout the trip. High trippers can be sure, however, that they will (1) move after two or three or four or five nights in one place; (2) remain two or more nights in the next camp whenever the pack trains, having unloaded dunnage and equipment, have to shuttle the food supplies; and (3) choose their own pace when they move, and their own companions—if any—on the trail.

The trips run consecutively for periods of about two weeks each.

On each two-week period there is ample opportunity for climbing, fishing, lazing, or organizing knapsacking side trips.

Since the High Trips have been going on the longest, they are richest in tradition. The prospective freshman would do well to ask an oldtimer about bandanna shows, trailside tea parties, mail, and indispensable extras not included in the official equipment check lists.

Small musical instruments and extra photographic supplies can usually be transported by special arrangement with the management.

Requirements of physical fitness are as necessary for the High Trip as for the Burro Trips, for the itinerary still entails exertion at high altitudes, even though the mules are chased by the packers. Members must also be prepared to volunteer help in camp tasks; the size of and compensation for the commissary crew, as well as the cost of the trip, are based on the assumption that members will help.

As a conservation measure, the High Trips now take far fewer members than they originally did. Although this is less economical (outing deposits are in consequence proportionally higher than in previous years), it is a necessary limitation because of the progressively increased grazing load upon the high mountain meadows. Therefore the Outing Committee does not feel justified in providing for such large parties as in past years. Few saddle animals will be available on a long-term basis; there will be some on hand, however, for emergency use at daily rates.

HIGH-LIGHT TRIP

The High-Light Trip is for those who enjoy a medium-sized trip (50 or fewer), who like to have their food and dunnage packed for them, and who enjoy mountain cookery and their turn at commissary chores. It is a traveling trip, moving almost every other day for two weeks and thereby covering considerable distance, affording access to more remote mountain areas. In effect the trip is a combination of Knapsack and High Trip techniques. Two packers with mules transport the dunnage bags (limited to 25 lbs. each), the commissary gear (stoves are eliminated), and the various lightweight dehydrated foodstuffs which are so dear to knapsackers' hearts.

A small leadership group instructs and coördinates the cook crews working in rotation and drawn from the membership of the trip. Everyone enters into the fun and camaraderie of working together. Because of the limited dunnage, the smaller staff, the light-weight food, this trip has proved to use fewer animals per man than any other travelling pack trip.

Also, as only two pack strings are required, this trip is versatile in the number of pack outfits it can call upon.

BASE CAMP

Those who prefer to explore intensively rather than extensively find the Base Camp, situated each year in some site not too far from a roadhead, a convenient way of meeting the problems of packing and commissary. A kitchen crew that can count on keeping its equipment in the same place and receiving fresh supplies at frequent intervals can—and does!—make a feature of varied and sumptuous menus, and Base Camp is noted for fine food. Each session—there are several when registration warrants—runs for two weeks.

Educational and entertainment features alike are stressed in campfire programs, and Base Camp, too, has its traditions—some adopted from High Trips, some developed in response to slightly different conditions. Leadership is arranged for short and long daytime trips in the vicinity of the camp.

Horses will be available for those who prefer to ride from the road end to the campsite, and tents may be reserved for those who prefer not to bring their own. Musical instruments and extra photographic supplies can usually be packed in free in excess of the usual dunnage limitations. Arrangements should be made in advance.

THE RIVER TRIPS

When the threat to build an Echo Park dam and flood Dinosaur National Monument was made, the Outing Committee was encouraged by David Brower and Harold Bradley to show the members this wonderful river canyon, hoping, as John Muir had hoped, that travelers would come back from this wilderness to fight for its preservation. Thus the river outings were born; the first of them, cautiously scheduled in 1953, were an overwhelming success.

About the same time but quite independently, a group of club members who had developed enthusiasm for foldboating formed themselves into a group which grew into a section of the San Francisco Bay Chapter. With the impetus of this group and the need for visiting our river wilderness areas, there is no end to future possibilities of exploration and successful river trips.

The River Trips offer one of the easiest ways of entering and enjoying the wilderness. Floating down the river in a rubber boat, viewing the sights and panoramas of passing cliffs, canyons and bottom lands, is an effortless way of visiting these otherwise inaccessible areas. Variation in the day's trip is afforded by a dip into the river or the thrill of passage through rapids. As experienced boatmen are in charge, no danger is encountered that cannot be adequately handled. When encountering rough water, it is mandatory to wear the float coats that are provided.

A commissary crew prepares the meals but the members are expected to volunteer for small tasks. As each day's journey ends at noon or shortly thereafter, sufficient time is left for exploration of side canyons or interesting phenomena along the way, as well as for fishing, swimming, or being lazy.

There are no physical qualifications for these trips. "All you have to do is to breathe," is the way Harold Bradley described the requirements. You do not even have to know how to swim, but the recommended minimum age is eight.

Trips to Wherever Wilderness Is

As the total program of the club enlarges, the necessity increases of spreading the outing program over the wilderness of many regions. Especially is this true when there are conservation battles to be fought. Also it has become increasingly clear that the peculiar biotic balance of the Sierra Nevada is extremely fragile, and spreading the load is helpful.

At first, Sierra-developed techniques were transported to the other states, but experience with weather, terrain, and packing facilities has shown that modification of our traditional trips is necessary for smoother operation. Instead of fitting the country to our trips, we try to fit the trips to the country. New types of trips are developing—base camps with packing assistance to outlying points, modified traveling trips, and combinations of these with knapsacking. The use of canned fuels instead of the indigenous wood supply, more tentage—these are some of the innovations. There will be more changes as well as more trips, so that our increasing membership can enjoy superb areas still new to the club— wherever there is wilderness to be explored, enjoyed, and protected for another generation to appreciate.

Each spring, an announcement of summer outings is published in one of the monthly *Bulletins*. Information is provided on routes, camps, cost, and other details. Copies of the latest outing announcement are usually available at the club office.

A printed leaflet, listing the clothing and equipment that members are advised to bring on the outings, may be obtained from the club office.

Lodges and Lands

I N THE COURSE of more than sixty years the Sierra Club has acquired property at various locations in the mountains of California. Its holdings include wild, undeveloped lands as well as lodges or huts, either on its own property or on sites leased from the government. Some parcels of land have been received as gifts, others have been purchased—either for the purpose of protecting certain important holdings from exploitation, or for use as building sites.

The various lodges serve as recreation centers—particularly for winter sports—for members and their guests, as centers of mountaineering information, or as emergency shelters.

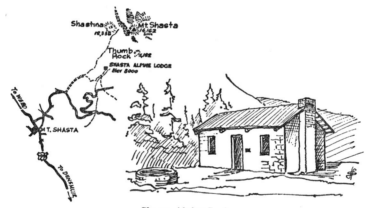

Shasta Alpine Lodge

The detailed management of the lodges and huts in the Donner Summit area is vested in the Clair Tappaan Lodge Committee, and that of the Harwood Lodge in the Angeles Chapter. All other lodges, huts, and lands are administered directly by the Committee on Lodges and Lands, which is also authorized to exercise control over matters of policy and general rules applicable to all lodges.

Following is a brief survey, from north to south, of where the lands and lodges are, and what they are like.

Shasta Alpine Lodge is situated on a 720-acre piece of club property at about 8,000 feet elevation (near timberline) on 14,161-foot Mount Shasta. It is a sturdy, one-room stone building, built in 1922 on an 80-acre piece purchased by the club; its construction was made possible largely through the generosity of a public-spirited club member, the late M. Hall McAllister. The lodge serves as an overnight stop for members or visitors desiring to climb the mountain. In the summer there is usually a custodian in residence, and camping space is available adjacent to the lodge. In the winter the lodge is left unlocked for use by skiers (first come, first in). Access is via the Everett Memorial Highway (unpaved) from Mount Shasta City to Sand Flat, and thence by 1½ miles of trail to the lodge, at Horse Camp. The additional 640 acres were purchased at a later

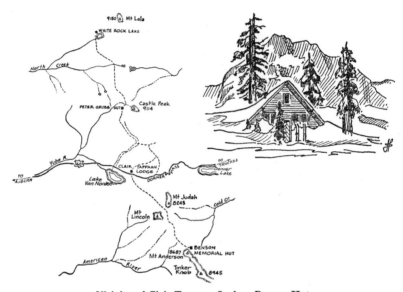

Vicinity of Clair Tappaan Lodge; Benson Hut

date to protect title to the lodge's water supply, and happen to comprise some of the finest ski terrain on the mountain.

Clair Tappaan Lodge is the club's largest establishment; built in 1934, it has been under almost constant expansion, remodeling, and improvement, all by volunteer labor. It is at an elevation of 7,000 feet near Norden, 1½ miles west of Donner Summit, on U. S. Highway 40. The lodge is a memorial to the late Judge Clair Sprague Tappaan, an enthusiastic member, one-time president, and for many years director, who did especially commendable work as assistant in the management of the outings and led in the forming and conducting of the Southern California (Angeles) Chapter. Although originally intended only for winter use by skiers, the Tappaan Lodge is becoming increasingly popular in the summer. A manager is now in residence the year around, and in the winter a professional cook is in charge of the well-equipped kitchen. Skiers assist in the "housekeeping" and take turns at dishwashing and other chores. The lodge includes a large living room, men's and women's dormitories and married couples' "cubicles," a large kitchen and dining room, a ski work room, first aid room, storage basements, and staff quarters. The lodge is on Forest Service land, but the club owns about 24 acres of near-by land on which there is a spring and on which the club's own ski tow and warming hut are situated.

Hutchinson Lodge, formerly the Sierra Ski Club, was acquired along with 67 acres of land in early 1956. It is at Norden, near Clair Tappaan Lodge. Hutchinson Lodge, with a capacity of 15, is reserved for independent groups of club members who are age 18 or over. The parties do their own cooking and housekeeping, thus keeping expenses to a minimum for skiing in the Donner Summit area.

Flora and Azalea lakes property, a 320-acre piece within easy strolling distance of Clair Tappaan Lodge, includes two charming mountain lakes.

Peter Grubb Hut, at 7,600 feet, in a little bowl below Castle Peak, is about 5 miles north of Clair Tappaan Lodge, and is a popular destination for day tours and for overnight ski trips. The original log-sided shelter was built in 1937 by friends of the skier and climber to whom it is a memorial. Today the larger stone-walled addition provides cooking facilities and bunks for about twenty people.

The *Benson Memorial Hut* was completed in 1949 as a memorial to club member John P. Benson who was killed in World War II. It is an architecturally pleasing building located at 8,350 feet elevation on the north slope of Mount Anderson (8,687 feet), 5 miles from Norden and 3 miles from the Cold Creek roadhead. It is built of stone to the window sills and timber above, and has 12 bunks.

Ludlow Ski Hut is also part of the chain being built by the club along the main crest of the Sierra, and is 16 miles south of Benson Hut (and six miles west of Chambers Lodge on Lake Tahoe). It is a memorial to Bill Ludlow, who was killed in the Korean campaign. Funds contributed by his friends and relatives were matched by the club to provide for the hut's cost. The building is of A-frame type, with a 20′ x 25′ main floor, and a smaller upper floor.

The *Bradley Hut* is the latest in the chain, and is on the route from Benson to Ludlow, lying just a short distance over the Sierra crest from

Squaw Valley. It is a memorial to Josephine Bradley, the late wife of former club president Professor Harold Bradley, herself a skier, and mother of seven skiing sons, three of whom are professors, five of whom have doctor's degrees, and six of whom are club members. Funds contributed by the family and friends were matched by the club. As with all the huts, construction was done by work parties of members.

The *Parsons Memorial Lodge,* on the club's Soda Springs property, west of Lembert Dome, in Tuolumne Meadows, was built in 1915. The stone building, a single large room with spacious fireplace, provides a meeting place and an emergency shelter, and serves as a source of mountaineering information for members and public alike. It is a testimonial to the splendid conservation and outing work of Edward Taylor Parsons, for many years a director of the club. On the surrounding property there are many choice campsites, available to members and their families, and

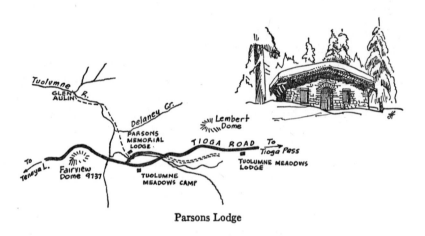

Parsons Lodge

during the summer custodians are in residence in the *McCauley Cabin,* which is adjacent to the lodge. Both lodge and cabin were exceptionally well improved by member Albert Duhme during his custodianship.

The *LeConte Memorial Lodge* in Yosemite was built in 1902–1903 in honor of Professor Joseph LeConte, the eminent scientist who was an early director of the Sierra Club and a great advocate of conservation, and who died in Yosemite Valley in 1901. It is now on the south side of the valley, about ¾ mile east of the Old Village, although it originally stood in what is now Camp Curry and was removed and rebuilt by the concessionaire to make room for an expanded Camp Curry. It served as the valley's only historical and scientific museum until the construction of the Park Service museum at Government Center. Today this, the oldest of the Sierra Club lodges, is visited by many of the general public, who find in its quiet atmosphere a small but growing mountaineering library, historic and educational collections of pictures, and a source of general information on conservation, the national parks, and the High Sierra. Here, too, is housed the Galen Clark library. It is appropriate that mileage southward along the John Muir Trail is reckoned from the LeConte Lodge, its northern terminus. This lodge offers its members no camping accommodations, but serves only as a gathering place. A custodian is in residence during the summer months.

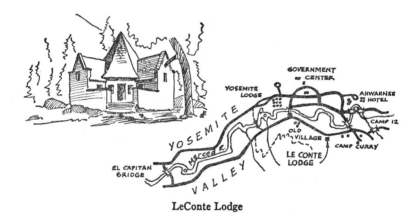

LeConte Lodge

Muir Shelter, at 12,059-foot Muir Pass (on the divide between the San Joaquin and Kings watersheds), is a stone hut of unique design, erected in honor of John Muir. It was built in 1930 by the Sierra Club with the aid of the Forest Service (on land which has since become a part of the Kings Canyon National Park), with funds donated by George Frederick Schwarz, a club member and an outstanding conservationist.

Zumwalt Meadow. On the floor of the Kings River Canyon (about 5,000 feet), the club owns about 70 acres of fine property given to the club by Jesse B. Agnew in 1923. The property is of particular interest and value, not only because of its location, but also because it is now protected from grazing and affords a charming example of natural meadowland. The club gave 13 acres of the original 80 to the National Park Service for a highway right of way after prolonged negotiation seeking to keep the highway as far as possible from Kings River at that point, so as to preserve a maximum of the river's edge for members of the public traveling on foot.

Harwood Memorial Lodge, at about 6,300 feet elevation in San Antonio Canyon (above Pomona), is a monument to the late Aurelia S. Harwood, who served as president and director of the Sierra Club, who was extremely active in conservation work and in the administration of the Southern California (Angeles) Chapter, and who donated a substantial sum to the furtherance of the club's objectives. This lodge was built and is administered by the Angeles Chapter, and since its completion in 1930 has been an increasingly popular week-end and vacation lodge. It has a well-equipped kitchen, dining room, lounge, and dormitories for men and

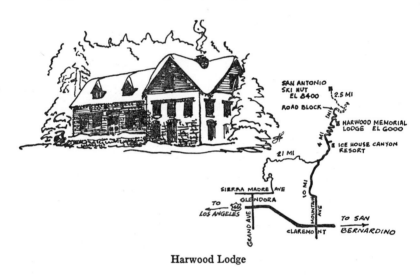

Harwood Lodge

women. Although there is no resident custodian, various members serve as host and hostess on week ends.

There was at one time the *Muir Lodge* in Big Santa Anita Canyon, built in 1913 and providing a delightful week-end and vacation spot, but it was so seriously damaged by a flash flood in 1938 that repair was impracticable, and the leased site was relinquished.

San Antonio Ski Hut, on Forest Service land at about 9,000 feet on the southern slope of 10,080-foot Mount San Antonio, is reached by a steep 2½-mile trail from the end of the road a short distance above Harwood Lodge. It was built by volunteer workers in 1935, but burned, and was rebuilt in 1936. It affords kitchen and bunk facilities for two dozen or so skiers.

The Guymon Cabins, on the Cleveland National Forest in San Diego County, were donated to the club by E. T. Guymon, Jr., in 1951.

Keller Peak Ski Hut, also built by skier-volunteers, is on Forest Service land on the Big Bear Highway in Snow Valley, at about 6,800 feet elevation, opposite Keller Peak. Built in 1938, it has a well-equipped kitchen, living room, small dining room, and dormitories. Although primarily a ski lodge, it is also used in the summer.

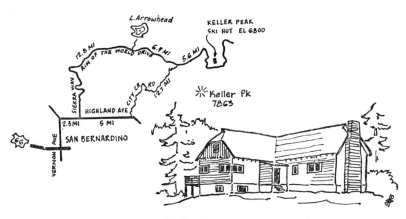

Keller Peak Hut

Winter Sports

THE SIERRA CLUB has long been interested in certain phases of winter sports although this activity was not one of the reasons for its formation. Individual members of the club recognized many years ago that the exploration and enjoyment of the Sierra Nevada is not confined to summer trips but is both feasible and rewarding in winter and spring as well. The official chronicles of the club testify to this. Early *Bulletins* at the turn of the century contained articles on the "Winter Sierra," "Mount Washington in Winter," and similar titles. The June, 1903, *Bulletin* tells how to make "skies" ranging from seven to twelve feet in length. J. E. Church, Jr., of the University of Nevada, wrote of his New Year outing in the Mount Rose region in January, 1901, and later of his climb high on Mount Whitney in March, 1905. He was fired with enthusiasm and a pioneering zest for exploration of the mountains in winter but he did not start out as a skier; on his early trips he used snowshoes and a homemade sled. Observing that "when it is considered that one must be a draught animal on such trips the uselessness of the ski is at once apparent." After contributing many interesting articles and notes to the *Bulletin* for more than a decade he finally acknowledged, in 1915, in his article describing "Lake Tahoe in Winter," that "skiing is the chief method of locomotion in winter at the lake."

As access to the snowbound Sierra became more practicable it was to be expected that the Sierra Club should lead in the encouragement of mountain touring in winter. Skis, which had been used in California since the days of "Snowshoe" Thompson, antedating the Pony Express, logically offered the most popular means of travel. Hazel King, with all the appreciation of a true skier, tells her impressions of ski running in the Tahoe country in the January, 1915, *Bulletin:* " . . . go to the mountain top . . . gather yourself together in a crouching position just as a bird does before it leaps into the air . . . you, too, will fly over that white world, alighting gradually and upright (we hope) . . . you have had the exhilaration of that wonderful downward movement, and after you have gathered yourself together again to reascend the slope, you have the pleasure in the climb . . . of speculating as to 'what is beyond that ridge' . . . until you find yourself once more at the top, ready and impatient to try again your ski wings."

If hers was one of the earliest tours, surely the longest was from Cottonwood Pass to Yosemite Valley on skis in a hundred days. How many of our ski mountaineers could do that High Sierra tour alone? So far as we know, only one man has—the late Orland Bartholomew, former member, completed his historic trip on April 3, 1929, and his illustrated account, together with scientific observations, appeared in the *Bulletin* of February, 1930. Editor Francis Farquhar wrote of it, " . . . That [this trip] marks the beginning of a new era . . . is apparent from the widespread interest in winter mountaineering manifested in the publications of other outdoor societies, and in the sport of ski-running . . . . With increased interest will come increased facilities. . . . Every Sierra peak will before long have its first winter-ascent, and with these climbs will come new experiences, new triumphs over difficulties, new unfoldment of the grandeur and beauty of our High Sierra."

Other club members were making unheralded ski tours in the mountains: Bestor Robinson, in a wide variety of terrain ranging from the Kaweah River to Castle Peak, Einar Nilsson in the Truckee country, Oliver Kehrlein in the Shasta and Lassen regions, Norman Clyde on the east slope of the Sierra, Clifford Hanchetts in the vicinity of Kearsarge Pass, Murray Kirkwood on Mount San Gorgonio. It would be impossible to name them all.

Beginning of the Winter Sports Committee

In the early thirties winter sports became organized in the Sierra Club. The December, 1929, *Bulletin* recorded the motion of the directors that "a committee be appointed to encourage among members of the club the use of the High Sierra for winter sports." President McDuffie appointed a committee which essayed to coördinate information from various parts of the Sierra on snow conditions, climate, camping facilities, and to "plan on a scheduled development of all phases of winter sport and travel in the Sierra . . . ." After some correspondence, the committee, consisting of Ansel Adams, chairman; Bestor Robinson, secretary; Oliver Kehrlein, Orland Bartholomew, and Frederick Reinhardt, met in December, 1930, and recommended that the Sierra Club "enter into a program for the encouragement of winter trips and expeditions into the Sierra Nevada back country" and leave the exploitation of snow sports at resorts to others. The advantages of various portions of the Sierra Nevada in winter were discussed and a seven-point program of recommendations was adopted, including a plan for making the timberline regions of the Sierra available for winter expeditions by the establishment of a series of inexpensive shelter cabins, separated by a distance that could be covered on skis in one day under adverse snow conditions.

About this time those interested in competitive skiing also felt the need of further organization, and in the fall of 1930 there was formed under the auspices of the winter sports committee of the California State Chamber of Commerce a "California Ski Association," comprising initially the following ski clubs: Truckee, Auburn, Yosemite, and Viking (Los Angeles). Their chief concern was the sanctioning of competitive ski meets. By the fall of 1936 the Ski Association had broadened its interests and the Sierra Club became a member and continued this affiliation until 1949. Then the Association (renamed Far West Ski Association) adopted revised by-laws under which the Sierra Club could not continue as a member club—until a later *re*revision.

By December 1932 the need for more than a study committee became apparent, and President Bernays appointed Francis Farquhar chairman of a committee to consider forming a Winter Sports Section of the club. Before Christmas a meeting was held, although the "season was already well advanced . . . to provide for some sort of classification of those participating in order that novices would not have to struggle to keep up with experts and experts be retarded by the company of novices . . . it was proposed that a system of grades be devised and that special attention be given to affording instruction so that members might move up from one grade to another. Another important matter was considered to be the recommendation of types of equipment and the explanation of their use . . . ." The committee organized itself into five subcommittees, with Bestor Robinson as chairman of the general committee and the following subcommittee heads: standards, Otto Barkan; equipment, Horace Breed; locations, C. A. Withington; trips, Lewis F. Clark; publications, Harold L. Paige.

EARLY TRIPS

In 1913 the club's first organized snow trip was made to Truckee. Guests went by train, sleeping and eating in Pullmans parked on a siding (with an engine hitched to maintain warmth), and used skis and snowshoes to explore the neighboring hills. A similar trip was made the following year but the pattern was not repeated. Over Washington's Birthday, 1931, the San Francisco Bay Chapter sponsored a "Snow Trip to Cisco" (three full days of winter sports in the land of snow). The Local Walks Committee picked Cisco from the map and selected Lewis Clark as leader of the trip because he had made a ski trip to Donner Summit one year previously; 1932 saw another Washington's Birthday trip to the Sierra snowfields, this time to Giant Forest, again under Clark's leadership. With the reorganization of the Winter Sports Committee in January, 1933, a schedule of ski trips was planned: to Camp Pahatsi (the Boy Scout lodge 3 miles west of Soda Springs) over February 11, 12, 13, and other, more informal trips to Cisco, Giant Forest, Yuba Pass, and Soda Springs. Starting a new season, club members from the Bay region and southern California gathered at the old Sentinel Hotel in Yosemite to ski at Badger Pass; the annual Bay Chapter snow trip was repeated in 1934 to Camp Pahatsi. By this time many club skiers were agreed that we ought to have our own headquarters instead of having to sleep in old railroad stations and barns. In the February '34 *Bulletin* Neill Wilson wrote of the "Plan for Sierra Club Ski Headquarters at Norden," and the directors in May authorized the Winter Sports Committee to proceed with raising funds, and with volunteer labor on the part of club members to construct the "Clair Tappaan Lodge." Ready for use, the lodge was dedicated by Mr. Colby, Sunday evening, December 30, 1934, with an audience of 100 including about 60 who filled the lodge bunks to capacity for the New Year's week end.

GROWTH OF SKIING IN THE CLUB

In California, where men have skied, more or less, for almost a century, interest in the sport picked up about 1933 and has been steadily increasing since then, aided undoubtedly by better access to the higher elevations, where reliable snow can be found for at least a quarter of the year. Naturally the interest has grown within the club, too. An accelerating factor has been the availability of the Clair Tappaan Lodge, situated in the center of excellent ski-touring country, high enough to have reliable snow, with good practice hills near by, and conveniently close to rail transportation and to a highway kept plowed throughout the snow season. Since its dedication the Clair Tappaan Lodge has been operated by a separate committee, comprising representatives from the winter sports group and the three central California chapters of the club. Patronage of members (mostly from the Bay region, but with increasing numbers from the South) has grown to the extent that the lodge now has a resident manager throughout the year, and a cook during the snow season, although housekeeping duties are shared by all members attending.

Consideration of growth of skiing in the club must include special mention of Dr. Joel Hildebrand, who in a comprehensive sense has fathered skiing in this region. A competent skier himself, father of four active skiers, ski teacher and coach, developer of ski tests and inventor of ski games, author of many articles on skiing, supporter of the winter sports program of the club, acknowledged across the nation as a leader in ski sport, Professor Hildebrand's widespread influence in encouraging members to learn how to ski and in maintaining high skiing standards can only be suggested.

SOUTHERN SECTION

From the first meetings of the Winter Sports Committee in 1930 it was recognized that there should be a group of club members to undertake in southern California activities similar to those proposed for northern California. At first the winter exploration activities were on an individual basis. In February, 1931, Nathan C. Clark and two University of Southern California students climbed Mount San Gorgonio afoot in a twenty-hour trudge, and separately Murray Kirkwood and a companion climbed the peak on skis. Leslie LaVelle, later a club ski-test judge, was developing a group of skiers at Big Pines. In 1932 there came to southern California one of the most energetic and eloquent of skiing enthusiasts, Dr. Walter Mosauer, a biologist at the University of California, Los Angeles. He began teaching the principles of the Arlberg technique, which he had learned in Austria, to students at U.C.L.A. and Pomona College. In 1933 Dr. Mosauer was appointed chairman of a southern California section of the Winter Sports Committee, which included also D. Ray Brothers, Nathan C. Clark, Glen Dawson, Donald de Fremery, and H. C. Youngquist. In 1934 Dr. Mosauer published one of California's first booklets on ski technique, *On Skis over the Mountains*. A group of college students in the South, including a number of club members, fired with Dr. Mosauer's contagious enthusiasm, organized the "Ski Mountaineers." In 1935 the Southern California (now Angeles) Chapter of the club approved the establishment of a Ski Mountaineers Section, which absorbed Mosauer's ski mountaineers and gained additional members for the club. The club Ski Mountaineers explored the airy ridges and steep canyons of Mount San Antonio, Telegraph Peak, Ontario Peak, and Blue Ridge, with the crowning experience of climbing the north wall of Mount San Gorgonio, southern California's highest mountain. It was soon realized that the elevation of the club's Harwood Lodge was too low for reliable skiing and so, to get a higher base, the Ski Mountaineers built a hut on the upper south slope of Mount San Antonio—the "Baldy" Hut,—every bit of material and furnishings being carried up the canyon on the backs of members. It was finished by December, 1935, but burned completely one Sunday night in the following September. The second San Antonio Hut was started immediately by the Ski Mountaineers, was ready for use that ski season and was finished in the spring of '37. Following Dr. Mosauer's death in Mexico in August, 1937, the Ski Mountaineers started a fund for the purpose of building a ski lodge in his memory, and they were hoping that a site on San Gorgonio could be obtained. When, in 1938, the Forest Service had definitely denied a permit for a San Gorgonio site, the Ski Mountaineers organized a committee under the chairmanship of George Bauwens to build a ski hut on the Rim-of-the-World Highway opposite Keller Peak. The Keller Peak Hut, used the next ski season, proved so popular that an addition was projected and completed in the fall of 1939. The Ski Mountaineers group was a nucleus for many of the younger club members who were interested in rock climbing as well as skiing and for some who were not devotees of either sport but who gravitated to the company of the group. They began on January 29, 1938, and have continued, the publication of the *Mugelnoos,* a mimeographed news periodical relating to the activities of skiers and rock climbers.

The Ski Mountaineers group has conducted many ski expeditions into the east side of the Sierra. Beginning with Dr. Mosauer's trip to Kearsarge Pass in April, 1933, they have explored most of the east-side canyons and slopes as far north as Conway Summit. The Ski Mountaineers as an organization conduct ski tests, seminars, sponsor ski races, and in general administer the winter sports program in southern California.

WHO ARE SKI MOUNTAINEERS, PER SE?

They are devotees of the grand sport that results when skiing and mountaineering are blended. Says the *Manual*: "The arena for this sport is almost boundless, extending beyond the skiways, through timberline country where the air seems to share the vigor of the peaks, where snows are tracked only by one's chosen friends. Such is the terrain that mountaineering gives abundantly to the skier." In the Sierra Club, ski mountaineers may be members of a section of the club, but more broadly they may be those regardless of residence who have passed the Ski Mountaineering Test, originated by the club and now established by the National Ski Association as an objective measure of the ability required for safe ski mountaineering, including proficiency at least as a third class skier, and demonstrated knowledge and skill in first aid and ski rescue, the basic principles of snowcraft and avalanche hazard, ability in map reading, snow camping and mountain touring on skis. Members of the club have played leading parts in developing this technique, reporting it, and compiling the *Manual of Ski Mountaineering*, first published in 1942 by the University of California Press and revised, with the benefit of war experience, in 1946 and 1947, and taken over by the club in 1960.

Some of the beginnings of ski mountaineering in the club have already been referred to in previous paragraphs. Many other expeditions have been made, some of them chronicled in the *Bulletin*: the first winter ascent of Mount Lyell and of Mount Clark in Yosemite, of the Bear Creek Spire, North Palisade, and others. Many are the tours undertaken and remembered by various groups just for the fun of it, with nothing for the record. It is one of the primary purposes of the Winter Sports Committee to encourage more of this, and to help members to acquire the skill and know-how so that they may enjoy ski mountaineering with safety and satisfaction.

THE WINTER-SPORTS PROGRAM

Further indication of the scope of activities of the Winter Sports Committee is outlined in the following highlights of its accomplishments:

Ski tests—Invented the ski-mountaineering and the 4th class ski tests; sponsored adoption of the present five grades of ski tests by the California Ski Association and the National Ski Association; has given ski tests to hundreds of club members.

Skiways—Developed the concept of skiways with the Forest Service; recommended routing and marking.

Publications—Contributed largely to the *Manual of Ski Mountaineering* and its revision; committee members have had numerous articles on skiing published in the *American Ski Annual* and other magazines; publication by the Ski Mountaineers Section, since January, 1938, of the mimeographed *Mugelnoos*.

Courses—Conducted ski mountaineering courses, with both discussion groups and field trips, in both southern California and central California, prewar and postwar.

Ski touring—Initiated many High Sierra ski tours and expeditions, as elsewhere described.

Lodging—Conceived and constructed the original unit of the Clair Tappaan Lodge, and assisted in its expansion; built the Peter Grubb Hut; initiated plans and coöperated with the Clair Tappan Lodge Committee in constructing the Benson Ski Cabin on Mount Anderson, the Ludlow Hut near Richardson Lake, and in the Josephine Bradley Hut, between the other two—all part of a master plan for a series of ski huts between Highways 40 and 50, on the crest of the Sierra west of Tahoe; promoted with the National Park Service the planning of Pear Lake Ski Hut in Sequoia National Park and the Ostrander Lake Ski Hut in Yosemite National Park. In southern California the Ski Mountaineers Section initiated and built the San Antonio Ski Hut and the Keller Peak Ski Hut.

Ski tow—Initiated and built the club ski tow on the west side of Signal Hill, near Norden, and a warming hut of celebrated architecture.

Equipment—Experimented with and tested various types of ski-mountaineering gear, and based on this experience contributed points of view and advice through several committee members who served in the Office of the Quartermaster General in Washington during the war years.

Ski patrol—Worked closely with the California Ski Association and the Army on ski-patrol war defense plans; maintained a club patrol unit of the National Ski Patrol System for a number of years.

Terrain survey—Began a survey of ski terrain in California, correlating information based on the explorations of many club members and augmented by aerial photographs taken in the ski season by Lowell Sumner.

Liaison—Maintained close liaison with the National Park Service and the Forest Service in studying ski recreation within and near national park and wilderness areas.

Ski instruction—In addition to the inestimable amount of individual coaching of members by their more expert friends, the club has benefited by having for some fifteen years the headquarters of the Klein Ski School at the Clair Tappan Lodge, and more recently its own school.

WORK PARTIES

It was as natural as the falling of snow for skiing club members—and their friends—who felt the need of a lodge or hut to organize a coöperative project. They recognized that each could contribute time and effort and whatever special skill he or she had. Brains, brawn, and spare cash got together. The Clair Tappaan Lodge and outpost huts, and the San Antonio and Keller Peak huts have one quality in common: they have been built by the combined work of many volunteers over the years. This spirit of coöperation is a precious tradition. Each member who uses one of these places can share in this tradition by doing his part in current maintenance, and by having fun and the satisfaction of accomplishment on summer work parties whose mission is to improve the facilities and eventually extend the chain.

Administration of the Club

THE GOVERNING body of the Sierra Club is the 15-man Board of Directors, elected annually by vote of the membership. At their organization meeting, held in May, the directors elect the President, Vice-President, Secretary, and Treasurer. These four officers, together with a fifth member chosen by the directors, constitute the Executive Committee.

The Board of Directors holds several meetings at intervals during the year. Members of the club are welcome at meetings of the Board.

Since 1953 the club has employed an Executive Director. From his desk in the San Francisco office, this official devotes his full time to carrying out the policies of the club as formulated by the Board of Directors. He makes trips to New York, Washington, and other cities to confer with other organizations, testifies at hearings and addresses various groups in behalf of the club, and exerts the influence of the Sierra Club in order to implement its aims, chiefly in the field of park and wilderness conservation.

Each chapter is officially represented at Board meetings, and also sends a delegate to meetings of the Sierra Club Council, as do the principal committees of the club. The Council was voted in 1956 to assist in administering the increasingly complex affairs of the club.

In nine areas of California, in the Great Basin, and in the Pacific Northwest and Atlantic coast areas, the twelve chapters carry out the club's purposes on a local or regional basis. Each chapter has its own version of the club's uniform by-laws for chapters, elects an executive committee, and conducts business related to conservation, outings, publicity, education, and social affairs. Chapters receive funds from the club treasury, but many local activities are self-supporting. Members are encouraged to attend executive committee and chapter meetings and to participate in the work of chapter committees. It is here that many receive their introduction to valuable opportunities for constructive effort.

The bulk of the club's work is volunteered by the many committees—more than 30 of them—whose chairmen are appointed by the President, with concurrence of the Board of Directors. Other articles in this *Handbook* tell the story of the committees and their vital contributions. Each has its role in making the Sierra Club, with its diversified program and more than 11,000 members, one of the leading conservation organizations of the United States.

"... the Sequoia of the Sierra was fortunate in having John Muir for a friend, and now it is the best-protected species of tree in the New World."

—WILLIAM R. DUDLEY, 1898

JOHN MUIR, FIRST PRESIDENT   *Dassonville*

Some Members
Through the Years

In nearly seventy years an organization like the Sierra Club can accumulate a staggering number of photographs, and that is what has happened. They range from fine prints to snapshots, from well-labeled data to complete mysteries. Within the collection are snapshots that probably should be winnowed out—except for the value they may have for important comparisons: For example, how much better off is this meadow now, seventy years later? Has the character of the forest changed, as viewed from the same spot? What has happened to the stream since logging set in? How far has the glacier receded? And is the granite as enduring as the poets say, or has part of this summit collapsed in this century? The collection, like wilderness, may hold the answers to questions we haven't yet thought to ask.

It is also a brutal collection, in a way, unkind in showing how unrelenting time can be with people, how vitality brims in the young peak climber, gives way to deeper and mellower qualities, then is replaced by something that is first venerated and finally forgotten. Which is merely to restate the final paragraph of Joseph LeConte's *Ramblings*: "Alas how transitory is . . . all earthly life, its elements gathered and organized for a brief space, full of enjoyment and adventure, but swiftly hastening to be again dissolved, and returned to the common fund from which it was drawn."

For all that, there is something very lasting about the kind of spirit that flows through the people who like mountains, from generation to generation, and will probably flow as long as the mountain habitat lives. Here, drawn almost at random from a vast store, and however imperfect, is a measure of that spirit.

Martinez, May 10, 1892

Mr. Henry Senger —

Dear Sir

I am greatly interested in the formation of an alpine club. I think with you & Mr. Olney that the time has come when such a club should be organized. You may count on me as a member & as willing to do all in my power to further the interest of such a club. I shall be glad to see you at my house near Martinez, or to meet you in the city. Mr. Armes of the State University — is also interested in the organization of such a club & I advise you to correspond with him.

Yours truly, John Muir

The
First
Decade
1892-1899

J OHN MUIR'S *letter led to the meeting that started the club on its way. The Soda Springs cabin in Tuolumne Meadows had a roof then, and the original Yosemite headquarters was built six years later where Camp Curry now is.*

M. Frank Strauss

Edward Taylor Parsons

Camping equipment was still simple on the floor of Yosemite Valley and was being enjoyed by Helen Gompertz, Anita Gompertz, Caroline LeConte, and J. N. LeConte, July 1897. Helen Gompertz became Helen LeConte. J. N. (Little Joe) LeConte became the club's first Honorary President.

His father, Professor Joseph LeConte, at the Vernal Fall Bridge, Yosemite, July 22, 1897, had published "Ramblings" 22 years earlier. The club Yosemite head-quarters was to be named in his honor. Contemporary conservationists were (below) Charles Keeler, John Muir, William Keith, Francis Fisher Browne, and John Burroughs.

The Second Decade

President Roosevelt met with John Muir in Yosemite in 1903 and learned further reasons for calling a Governor's Conference. The annual outings started and wandered afield as far as Mount Rainier (the party, including Stephen Mather, assembled by the hotel in Portland in 1905). There was still a Hetch Hetchy Valley, in which the 1906 packers enjoyed a bit of horseplay. John Muir was studying Arizona's Petrified Forest that same year, and guiding the first tourists to see it. A lad who would serve longest as editor of the Bulletin was repeating an ascent of his first peak in 1903—Francis Farquhar (left) on Saddleback Mountain, Maine. The year before that there had been dancers on the floor of Kings Canyon, where Little Joe Le-Conte photographed them on the second Annual Outing in 1902.

The Teen Years

The same trail seemed steeper to some people as the outings, in 1911, probed back of Yosemite, planted trout in barren Sierra lakes, took their last look at Hetch Hetchy Valley as it could have remained, and rode out through the Tuolumne Grove. The Tioga Road was hard put to carry even wagons then, and sheep were still overgraz-

Photos by
C. H. Hamilton

E. T. Parsons

*ing outside Yosemite's bound-
ary near Alger Lake. An early
outing leader, Edward Taylor
Parsons, died suddenly, and a
lodge was built in his memory
in 1915, its door looking out on
Tuolumne Meadows country
he loved. A young Will Colby,
in his eleventh year of outing
leadership, caught more and
bigger trout than one is likely
to find in Yosemite these days.*

Marion Randall Parsons

Herbert W. Gleason

Ansel Adams

The 'Twenties

The Outing, meaning then the High Trip, was still the thing, and names became firmly embedded in the club's High Sierra tradition. A new photographer dropped by camp in Kings Canyon in 1925 and tried his hand, catching another photographer, Cedric Wright, with violin. Little Joe LeConte was there, and three other club presidents with him—Will Colby, Robert M. Price, and Tap (Judge Clair S. Tappaan), for whom a major lodge was to be named within a decade. Two years later Ansel Adams found four Colbys all together—a pass, William E., and sons Gilbert and Henry. This was a decade that had begun with a difficult climb, the first ascent of Middle Palisade, and the next day, August 27, 1921, the pair who made it were happy—Ansel Hall and Francis Farquhar. Farquhar had warmed up the year before on Mount Haeckel, where he photographed Walter Huber, who would be the seventh president, on top.

C. O. Schneider

Ansel Adams

Francis Farquhar

Photos by Ansel Adams

The 'Thirties

*Hovering somewhere around those frosty morn-
ings—above them, or just ahead of them—was a
growing knowledge that outings in wilderness were
something that just had to keep going on. In 1936
a young medical student, Stewart Kimball, seemed
pleasantly unaware that most of the outing burden
would one day be his, but Will Colby must have
known that he would have respite. Why else the
smile of relief?*

*Smiles of relief mixed with fatigue came that
same decade on the faces of Bestor Robinson,
Dick Leonard, and Jules Eichorn when they became first to the top of the High Cathedral Spire
in Yosemite, breaking a new barrier in American
rock climbing. If there was also anxiety in their
smiles, it must have been about the rappel which
lay ahead of them, and no one will ever get a finer
photograph of rappelling than the one of Jules
Eichorn, on the Lower Spire in 1937, by Dick
Leonard, who, once back on easier ground, would
serve as outing leader for ten years and become
the 21st president. But a war and twenty years
must pass first.*

Photos by Richard Leonard

The 'Forties

New things were happening along the high-mountain route. It had been found, mapped, sketched, and photographed, and now Leland Curtis was painting, and a High Trip audience admiring, what he discovered in the new Kings Canyon National Park the route led to. Two of the route's discoverers—Duncan McDuffie, the club's ninth president, and Little Joe LeConte, the second president—were photographed almost for the last time as the decade ended. They died early in the next one. The ranks of the pioneers were thinning.

Anonymous

Ansel Adams

Anonymous

Joel Hildebrand

New routes were being marked: The Sierra Crest hut and trail system was emanating from Clair Tappaan Lodge, now in its own second decade. Courses for competitive skiers—in this case a slalom on Mount Lassen. In summer the marks were sometimes on the feet of the user, and a High Trip blister fixer (medical student John Blosser, in '41) would go to work by the aid tent. The club's 23d president, Harold Bradley, took a last look at a trail the re-aligned Tioga Road would make obsolete—a trail built to fit the terrain by Gabriel Sovulewsky in the old days. There were field conferences about routes, including one along the shores of Tenaya Lake in '49 (shown here, Tom Carpenter and Thomas Vint of the National Park Service, with David Brower), which the Sierra Club hoped to spare from the ravages of a high-speed mountain route.

Cedric Wright
Harold Bradley

David Brower

The 'Fifties Were Busy

There were more Board meetings now. Some formal; some informal (as at Walter Starr's place near Mission Peak—Starr, Arthur Blake, Lewis Clark); and some semiformal, as in 1956 outside LeConte Lodge (Brower, Alex Hildebrand, Clark). Films were made, including "Two Yosemites," the story of the Hetch Hetchy yosemite that was lost.

Harold Bradley

¶ *More huts and lodges were added to the system: Hutchinson Lodge, the Signal Hill Warming Hut, the Benson, Bradley, and Ludlow memorial ski-touring huts (Ludlow hut shown, with Boss-builder Ned Robinson and slaves Bestor, Merritt, and Warren Robinson). Meanwhile, out on the ski slopes, Father Time got hung up in the slalom flags trying to catch Professor Joel Hildebrand, 13th president.* ¶ *The load on the Sierra increased and clean-up outings were started. (We even studied new packing methods to*

William Siri

Philip Hyde

Rondal Partridge

Ansel Adams

Cedric Wright

Christine Reid
William Siri

ease the impact on meadows, and trained
smaller fishermen to catch the smaller trout
the Sierra was now producing!) ¶ Out in the
vertical wilderness, war-born equipment—
better pitons and carabiners, nylon rope—
pushed horizons back. The Lost Arrow fell
further, and then the faces of Half Dome
and El Capitan. Outings went farther; expeditions too, as far as the Himalaya and
Makalu. Born of all this energy, the conservation force grew steadily. But the first
seven decades, rich and exciting, had not
been long enough.

Cedric Wright

Cedric Wright

WILLIAM E. COLBY AT BIG SUR, ABOUT 1957

*. . . and for six of the club's seven decades, the
national parks, the wilderness, the Sierra,
and the Sierra Club have been fortunate in
having a friend, too—a bold one, ready
and willing to fight in behalf of the
decades and the people yet to come.*

Trails

THE TRAIL ROUTES into and across the Sierra Nevada found by early American pioneers were those which had long been used by Indians. The mountains had not been explored or entered by the Californians living near the coast during the earlier period of Spanish and Mexican occupation. These Indian trails evidently afforded means for crossing the mountains for the purpose of trading between tribes living east and west of the range, and perhaps for the less peaceful purpose of raids by the more warlike Indians of the eastern side.

To cross the northern part of the High Sierra region, the Mono Trail ascended the western slope of the mountains from Mariposa via Wawona and Alder Creek to the meadows of Bridalveil Creek, where the trail forked. A branch descended to Yosemite Valley via Inspiration Point. The Mono Trail descended to Mono Meadow, crossed Illilouette Creek and ascended to Starr King Meadow, where it turned back at the rim of Little Yosemite to descend to the Merced River which it crossed about one mile above Nevada Fall. From there to Tuolumne Meadows the trail followed the present route of the Sunrise and Soda Springs Trail (the John Muir Trail route from Yosemite to Tuolumne Meadows). The old Indian trail then ascended the Dana Fork of the Tuolumne River to cross over (northern) Mono Pass south of Mount Gibbs and descended Bloody Canyon to Mono Lake, in the land of the Mono Tribe of Indians.

Owens Valley was the home of Piute Indians. They used (southern) Mono Pass, Piute Pass and Kearsarge Pass to cross the range on the routes of the present trails.

While the early mining prospectors used and improved these trails, and built a few others, it was the sheep and cattle men who were responsible for much of the trail system of the Sierra Nevada, especially on its western slope. Excepting parts of the John Muir Trail, the High Sierra Trail, and some laterals which have been improved or relocated, most of the Sierra trails just happened—in moving livestock to and from summer ranges in high mountain meadows.

In Yosemite National Park, especially in the Tuolumne River watershed, United States Cavalry troops cleared and improved many of the cattle trails by use, and located some new trails, while on patrol duty in protecting Yosemite's back country before the National Park Service came into being.

Soon after organization of the Sierra Club in 1892, Theodore S. Solomons conceived the idea of a trail along the backbone of the High Sierra, keeping as near to the crest as possible. As already noted, the existing trails crossed the range. Rugged canyons and passes rendered a trail along the range difficult. From 1892 to 1897 Solomons with other members of the Sierra Club made extended trips of exploration, principally in the upper branches of the San Joaquin River and headwaters of the Merced.

In 1898 Joseph N. LeConte took up the quest for a High Sierra trail route. For many years thereafter, assisted by a few other members of the Sierra Club, he explored the canyons and the passes of the Kings and the Kern, and climbed many of the peaks along the crest.

In 1914 a committee of its members was appointed by the Sierra Club to enlist the help and coöperation of the State of California in the construction of a High Sierra Trail along the range. This committee was composed of Meyer Lissner (chairman), Walter L. Huber, David P. Barrows, Vernon L. Kellogg, and Clair S. Tappaan. Soon thereafter the President of the Sierra Club, John Muir, died, and it was decided to name the proposed trail "The John Muir Trail" as a fitting memorial. As a result of the efforts of the committee the California State Legislature made its first appropriation of $10,000 to finance work on the trail in 1915.

The responsibility of selecting the route and spending the funds was given to the State Engineer, Wilbur F. McClure. Basing his decision on the information obtained by the many explorations of the past twenty years, principally by members of the Sierra Club, as well as on observations of his own made in the field, McClure selected the route now followed by the completed trail as the official route of the John Muir Trail from Yosemite Valley to Mount Whitney. To solve the problems of trail construction he wisely secured the coöperation of the Forest Service and arranged to have actual trail construction done under the management and supervision of its officers. This the men of the Forest Service accomplished through the years, faithfully and efficiently, with the meager funds at their disposal for such a large undertaking. Additional appropriations of $10,000 were made by the legislature in each of the years 1917, 1925, 1927, and 1929 as the result of Sierra Club efforts. Here ended the era of State assistance in the building of the John Muir Trail.

To complete the trail on its official route there now remained two sections to be constructed over difficult passes. One of them, from the Kings to the Kern over Foresters Pass, was completed in 1932 by the National Park Service on the Kern River side of the divide and by the Forest Service on the Kings River side. The last section, up Palisade Creek at the headwaters of the Middle Fork of Kings River and over

Mather Pass to the headwaters of the South Fork of Kings River, was completed in 1938 by the Forest Service as the result of an appeal made to Regional Forester S. B. Show by the High Sierra Trails Committee of the Sierra Club, through its chairman. Forest Supervisors Booth, Benedict, and Elliott, of the Inyo, Sierra, and Sequoia national forests, coöperated to accomplish this work. Shortly thereafter the region containing this section of the trail was transferred to the jurisdiction of the National Park Service by the creation of Kings Canyon National Park. Thus the John Muir Trail finally became a reality more than forty years after it was first conceived.

Another important trail to render the high mountain regions of the Kern and the Kaweah accessible, was built in 1930–1931 by the National Park Service in Sequoia National Park under the supervision of Superintendent John R. White. Known as the High Sierra Trail, it starts at Crescent Meadow in Giant Forest, crosses the Kern-Kaweah divide to Kern River, meets the John Muir Trail on Wallace Creek tributary and proceeds to Mount Whitney by that route.

The trails of the High Sierra are now the responsibility of the National Park Service and the Forest Service. The work to be done each year on maintenance is most important. Both services have always lacked sufficient funds, earmarked in their budgets for trail maintenance, to do the job of keeping the trails decently passable. The Sierra Club wishes to coöperate with the services by making efforts to have the needed funds made available, and by reporting where it finds trail repairs to be most necessary. Individuals can help in this effort by noting where trails are washed out, blocked by fallen trees, or otherwise badly in need of repair, while out on their summer trips, and on their return report the information to the chairman of the Trails Committee of the Sierra Club. The leaders of the various outings should make such a report. The Trails Committee can then screen and consolidate the reports received and convey the information gathered to the Forest Service and the National Park Service for their attention.

Naturally, the standards of trails in the Sierra trail system differ greatly and consideration must be given to their origin as described. On some of the main routes of travel, especially where trails have been made or relocated by the Park Service or Forest Service, standards are generally fairly good, but on many laterals and secondary trails such standards should not be expected. Parties traveling over the trails can help to maintain them by staying on the trail and not making short cuts, especially on switchbacks. Few realize the harm done by this practice. Maintenance can also be greatly helped by removing, if possible, obstacles when met, instead of going around them.

One of the original purposes of the Sierra Club was to render mountain regions accessible. The club feels that this purpose has now been accomplished; that no more roads should be constructed in the wilderness area of the High Sierra extending from Yosemite National Park to Walker Pass; and that, with very few possible exceptions, no more trails should be constructed. To future generations of mountaineers should be left the pleasure, thrill, and experience of pioneering and finding their own routes to the many high mountain basins, lakes, and peaks which abound in this great wilderness.

THE NEED FOR TRANQUILITY

FOR A NATION that grows more metropolitan and industrialized every year, the experience of solitude, even the simple fact of quiet, has become inestimable . . . It is imperative to maintain portions of the wilderness untouched, so that a tree will rot where it falls, a waterfall will pour its curve without generating electricity, a trumpeter swan may float on uncontaminated water—and moderns may at least see what their ancestors knew in their nerves and blood.

BERNARD DEVOTO

The Sierra Club and Science

IT IS inevitable that an organization whose members enjoy and seek to preserve the wilderness should be drawn to the natural sciences. Our publications, campfire talks, and educational programs attest to our conviction that it is the versatile and informed lay scientist who is able to derive the greatest rewards from his outdoor experiences. The mountains take him into their confidence and he becomes a participant in a great adventure, rather than a dumbfounded spectator of something beyond his full comprehension.

In recent years the Angeles and San Francisco Bay chapters of the club have organized natural-science sections for the purpose of becoming more familiar with the fauna and flora of the local regions and of the Sierra Nevada. In the south this has been accomplished by special lectures and field trips. In the north, field work and lectures have been supplemented by study groups in astronomy, botany, entomology, geology, and marine zoölogy under competent leadership. Also, mimeographed *Nature Notes* have been issued which pertain to astronomy, the botany and ornithology of the Bay region, the trees of the Sierra Nevada, and plant lists for areas adjacent to the club lodges at Norden and Tuolumne Meadows.

Throughout its existence the Sierra Club has published in its *Bulletin* scientific writings of specialists in various phases of the natural history of the Sierra. Especially numerous are the geological papers in which the history, structure, and sculpturing of the range are described by such eminent and scholarly observers as John Muir, Joseph LeConte, Grove Karl Gilbert, and François Matthes. Zoölogical studies on butterflies, birds, and mammals have been contributed by Vernon L. Kellogg, Laurence I. Hewes, William F. Badè, Cornelius B. Bradley, and Joseph Grinnell. The botany of the Sierra and other California ranges has been admirably handled by such well-known students of western plants as William R. Dudley, Alice Eastwood, Willis L. Jepson, John G. Lemmon, Walter Mulford, and William A. Setchell. During the years, numerous important meteorological papers were presented by J. E. Church, Jr., and Alexander McAdie. William A. Brewer contributed an article on Cataract (Havasu) Canyon in Arizona and C. Hart Merriam wrote on the Indian villages of Yosemite Valley, while several shorter notices were done by David Starr Jordan. Ynes Mexía, noted botanical collector, contributed articles on Ecuador and the Amazon. More recently John Thomas Howell has contributed articles on the Sierra flora, and Lowell Sumner and

Richard M. Leonard have made a valuable analysis of factors affecting mountain meadows. Leonard and Werner Grob have contributed studies of snow avalanches.

Several club and chapter committees and subcommittees draw heavily upon natural history in their programs for entertainment and conservation education, and the outing leaders have not overlooked their opportunities to teach natural history where it is most inspiring and best illustrated.

Most of these studies are somewhat on the popular side, as they should be, but they give "authentic information" on the "mountain regions of the Pacific Coast"; and in a broad interpretation of the words, these studies may also be said to promote and fulfill an intellectual phase of the first stated purpose, so far as the scientific treasures of our mountains are concerned: "to explore and enjoy."

The Sierra Club is also dependent upon science in another way. A deep and unselfish concern for the future of wilderness as a natural resource may be relied upon to determine club policy upon such conservation problems as lie clearly within the province of experience and common sense, but the counsel of experts is essential to the adequate evaluation of matters involving forest, range, or wildlife management, or to predict the impact which any of civilization's grasping tentacles may have upon an unspoiled place of beauty. Sierra Club leaders must often consult scientists and scientific writings in order to implement forceful campaigns based upon well-considered and well-advised conservation policy.

In 1948, the Natural Sciences Committee was added to the standing committees of the club. Its members advise the Board of Directors upon such matters as may be referred to them for study. The committee assists the editor of the *Bulletin* in obtaining authoritative scientific articles for the club publications and it performs other duties as well. Recognizing the importance of continued and correlated field studies in glaciology, the club organized, in 1933, a standing committee on Glacier Study under the chairmanship of Oliver Kehrlein. Snowfield and glacier data have been collected which give much information concerning the expansion or contraction of the small Sierra glaciers that are the present-day remnants of once-great ice streams. This committee is now a subcommittee of the Natural Sciences Committee, as is also the Sierra Bighorn Committee, which was organized in 1941 under the guidance of Arthur H. Blake to investigate the status of the remaining Sierra bands of mountain sheep. Fred L. Jones has also headed the subcommittee (his extended field study was published in the 1950 annual *Bulletin*).

Several decades ago when the higher and more remote parts of the Sierra Nevada were not so readily accessible as they are today, the annual High Trips gave scientists the means to make observations and collections that otherwise could not have been made or only at much greater inconvenience and expense. Such, for example, was the opportunity available to Professor Willis L. Jepson, who accompanied the club through the Yosemite National Park in 1911 and to the Kern River Canyon in 1912. The plant collections obtained on those trips not only served Jepson in the preparation of his *Flora of California,* but the fruitful examination of the Yosemite collections is also acknowledged with gratitude by Dr. Harvey M. Hall in his *Yosemite Flora.*

In 1940 the club inaugurated the Base Camp outings which are particularly appropriate for students who may wish to make an intensive study of a limited area of the High Sierra rather than the broader reconnaissance type of survey that can be done on the High Trip. On these outings, camp facilities are established for ten days or two weeks in a favored locality in the subalpine zone, affording natural-science students ample time to investigate the geology, zoölogy, and botany of the region. The discovery of fossilized invertebrates in metamorphosed sediments at Garnet Lake on the 1941 Base Camp, and the important data on the distribution of Sierra plants obtained by John Thomas Howell have been particularly significant.

Many scientists have a much deeper interest in the activities of the Sierra Club than could be engendered by convenient access to mountain collecting stations. The natural sciences have largely passed through the descriptive "what" stage, and, coming of age, are asking "why" and "how" questions which take them into the field, not to collect, but to observe. The student of natural history can count scale-rows and calculate standard deviations at his office desk, but he has come to think of a species as a wild population, not as a museum specimen. The systematist and ecologist need to know how plants and animals behave before their habitats have been ravaged or "improved" by the heavy hand of man. These men value wilderness as an invaluable laboratory which cannot be duplicated if once destroyed. Thus the Sierra Club and the natural sciences are able to assist each other in the common effort to preserve for posterity natural features and wilderness values of inestimable worth to man and to science.

It is too early for good perspective, but it may well be that the club's greatest contribution to its scientific objectives began with the Fifth Biennial Wilderness Conference, held in San Francisco in 1957, and continued and expanded in the Sixth, the theme of which was "The Meaning of Wilderness to Science." The Fifth Conference drew chiefs from the principal bureaus administering the federal wilderness reserves and produced some notable papers, published in the 1957 Annual under the title, "Wildlands in Our Civilization." The Sixth brought international participation, thanks to financial assistance from Resources for the Future and the Conservation Foundation. For the first time in all the conferences, the full proceedings were published as an illustrated book, *The Meaning of Wilderness to Science.* This conference made it alarmingly clear that the most important source of the vital organic forms constituting the chain of life is the gene bank that exists in wilderness, where the life force has gone on since the beginning uninterrupted by man and his technology —and that for this reason alone it is important that the remnants of wilderness which still exist on our public lands should be preserved by the best methods our form of government can find.

The Library

THE SIERRA CLUB LIBRARY, maintained at the club rooms in San Francisco, contains books and periodicals in many fields, principally mountaineering, skiing, natural history, and conservation.

At the present time there are approximately 1,300 volumes in the library, as well as more than 125 sets of periodicals and many federal and state publications. The club exchanges its *Bulletin* for the periodicals of the principal mountaineering and ski clubs from all over the world, and this exchange material is bound and preserved carefully. New books, sent by publishers for review in the *Bulletin,* are added to the library, and many valuable items have been given to the club by its members and friends.

Of special value are the accessions relating to John Muir. These include Muir's letters to Robert Underwood Johnson and others concerning the creation of Yosemite National Park, received by the club through the generosity of the late Albert M. Bender, Dr. Harold Crowe, and William E. Colby. Also in the library are early issues of *Overland Monthly, Century Magazine,* and *Scribner's* containing Muir articles. Louise Million gave the library an autographed copy of the first edition of *The Mountains of California,* and the club has the other works of Muir, often in several editions. The library contains a few of the very rare complete original sets of the *Sierra Club Bulletin.* Among other interesting possessions are *Portfolio of the Mammoth Tree Grove* (Calaveras Grove), published in 1862, and a first edition of Professor Joseph LeConte's *Ramblings Through the High Sierra.* The gifts of many club members, and especially of Francis P. Farquhar and Glen Dawson, have helped to make this a very good mountaineering library, and it is unfortunate that space does not permit a more complete listing of these accessions, or of the many important mountaineering and ski-mountaineering additions acquired by Sierrans during World War II.

The Sierra Club Library was established in 1892; about 500 volumes had been accumulated at the club rooms in the Mills Building by April, 1906. The great fire destroyed the entire library as well as all records of the club and all its copies of the *Sierra Club Bulletin.* Expressions of sympathy and offers of help were received by the club secretary from all corners of the world. Edward Whymper, an honorary member of the club, wrote from London:

" . . . I hasten to assure you of my entire sympathy. The Club has been tried by fire, but it will, I hope and believe, emerge from the ordeal stronger than before.

"If I can, by sending you copies of my own books, or can in any other way assist in the restoration of your library, you have only to command me."

Similar response was received from the Mazamas, the Appalachian Mountain Club, the Alpine Club, and many individuals. By the fall of 1907 the library was reëstablished at the Mills Building club rooms. It has been expanding ever since.

The library is administered by a committee responsible to the directors of the club. The committee holds administrative meetings monthly, but the work of classifying and cataloguing of accessions, binding, mending, cleaning—and many other activities keep the librarians well occupied at work meetings held every Tuesday evening in the club rooms. A collection that was formerly inadequately preserved and classified is being protected for the future as well as being made available to present-day members. Following usual club policy, the library work is performed entirely on a voluntary basis and the Library Committee always is searching for added help in this important Sierra Club activity. Members are urged to assist at the weekly meetings of the committee, irrespective of whether they have had any previous library training.

Perhaps the most ambitious undertaking of the committee is the card catalogue now in preparation. The bulk of the volumes in the library have been catalogued by the Library of Congress card system and the librarians are in the process of classifying the club's collection of periodicals and compiling an analytical (article by article) set of cards for the *Sierra Club Bulletin*. All publications are placed on the shelves in accordance with the Dewey-decimal classification system.

In addition to books, periodicals and certain pamphlets, the collections of photographs and maps are the responsibility of the committee. The photographic collection is outstanding and the committee is cataloguing the photographs and albums, a difficult and lengthy task. On the other hand, the collection of maps is inadequate and it is hoped that it will be built up within the next few years.

Among the photograph albums are Ansel Adams', Cedric Wright's, and Philip Hyde's photographs, many of which constitute vivid records of the annual outings. Then there are four volumes of photographs printed for the club by Ansel Adams from the negatives made by Joseph N. LeConte on his early trips in the Sierra. Many other albums of High Trip photographs and mountain scenes will be readily available when their classification has been completed. The Frederick Morley Memorial

Collection of photographs likewise has proved of great interest. This collection was purchased by the club with funds provided by Mrs. Morley, in memory of her husband, who lost his life in 1921 while climbing the Cockscomb, near Tuolumne Meadows. Many of the photographs are by Vittorio Sella; several are the work of Fred Boissonnas. The club also has a collection of Mexican scenes, given by the Club de Exploraciones de Mexico. Two outstanding gifts to the club are the Sierra negatives of J. N. LeConte and Cedric Wright. Prints may be examined in the library but the catalogued negatives themselves are in a bank vault.

There are a number of valuable paintings at the club rooms, the dominant one being that of Mount Assiniboine, by Breuer, given by William E. Colby. Among other gifts from Mr. Colby are an original Audubon print and a painting by William Keith. The exhibits at the club also include Ferdinand Burgdorff's painting of a Sierra skyline, presented by the artist; Albert Bierstadt's mountain scene in the Kearsarge region, a painting presented to the club by the late Albert M. Bender; two Yosemite paintings, one by Chris Jorgensen and one by Thomas Hill; and a striking photo-mural of Mount St. Elias by Bradford Washburn.

In addition to the principal library in San Francisco, the club maintains a number of smaller libraries. Several years ago the Angeles Chapter established a library in the Los Angeles office, and its library committee and the club committee are in the process of developing a policy to cover both libraries. The need of an adequate library in southern California is apparent. The club also has a mountaineering collection at the LeConte Memorial Lodge, in Yosemite Valley, and some volumes are available at Parsons Memorial Lodge in Tuolumne Meadows and at Clair Tappaan Lodge, Norden. The committee hopes to build the library in San Francisco into an outstanding reference library in all of the fields which concern the club and at the same time to make duplicate or specialized materials available to the other libraries.

Conservation on Film

THE POWERFUL medium of the color motion picture was added to the Sierra Club's educational program in 1939, and a growing collection of color slides now provides further program material. Before the visual education project was started (offering armchair education), the various summer and winter outings enabled hundreds of persons to know the mountains intimately and in turn to spread the word of what they had seen and learned, but it became necessary to recruit the aid of more conservationists than could ever be brought into the mountains. Isolated public meetings and publications were not enough. Somehow the mountains must be brought to Mahomet.

By means of the club's 16mm. color motion pictures, vivid glimpses of the Sierra have been shown to thousands who had never been reached before. The success of the early pictures, described below, has led to plans for further films, and it is the hope of the Visual Education Committee to produce and distribute many new pictures of mountain travel.

Sky-Land Trails of the Kings, photographed in Kings Canyon National Park by Brower and Leonard, was first of the films, and came into being as a result of a report that during the hearings on the Gearhart Bill for formation of the park a senator pointed out that none of his colleagues had never seen the country in question and it might be a pig in a poke. A small appropriation by the club permitted two thousand feet of color film to be shot during the 1939 High Trip, and a preliminary edition of the film was shown in Washington where it would do—and did—the most good. The film was further edited, and showings in the course of the following winter brought in enough revenue for more film. Another two thousand feet were shot in 1940, and the total footage was edited down into the present 50-minute silent film, which is still in demand. It has been shown before groups ranging in content from Steig's Small Fry to Helen Hokinson's Best Girls, to students from grammar school to university level, and seems somehow to produce essentially the same audience reaction whatever the group.

Skis to the Sky-Land, completed in 1942, is a 50-minute silent color film comprised of scenes from two winters' ski mountaineering trips in the Sierra by its photographers, Brower, Lewis and Nathan Clark, and Leonard. This film had no legislative cause to serve, but it does seek to show that there is a more dramatic form of skiing than the common merry-go-round of riding up and sliding down one resort's practice hills—and that ski mountaineering is possible for all skiers who can carry a moderate pack and who are reasonably good skiers.

The picture shows many of the fine week-end touring areas in California, from Shasta to Sequoia. The major part of the picture, however, concerns itself with the first winter ascent of 13,705-foot Bear Creek Spire, situated at the head of what is probably the finest ski-mountaineering terrain in the Sierra; this was photographed in the course of two one-week expeditions, on which the size of the party ranged from fourteen to twenty-two. Much of the how-to-do-it of camping on snow is portrayed, showing in detail the various kinds of equipment that ski mountaineers enjoy experimenting with, and climaxing in downhill runs over spectacularly open slopes of April powder snow. The film proves that this is a sport for women as well as men.

Babes in the Woods, filmed by Leonard in 1947-49, is a 28-minute color picture to which a sound track is being added, showing the adventures of a mother and three young children on a small private burro trip. The techniques of burro packing and camp housekeeping, as well as the diversions enjoyed by the children, and a beautiful scenic background, make this a delightful picture for showing to any audience.

Wilderness River Trail, photographed by Charles Eggert, Martin Litton, and Nathan Clark in 1953, is a 28-minute color and sound picture recording highlights of the first season of river trips in Dinosaur National Monument, and showing why this spectacular unit of our national parks must not be impaired by dams or other destructive developments. It follows adventures of campers of all ages as they glide under brilliant cliffs or run the rapids thrillingly but safely in rubber rafts (or foldboats for the bold). Eggert's narration emphasizes the importance of park protection; music by Clair Leonard enhances the impressive scenic features.

Two Yosemites, photographed by David R. Brower in 1955, is a ten-minute film in color and sound showing the contrast between the once lovely valley of Hetch Hetchy (considered by many almost a rival to Yosemite in natural beauty), now a dreary travesty of a "recreational area," and the still living waters of Yosemite itself. The lesson of this film—that if Hetch Hetchy had been left in its original state and the Tuolumne River dammed farther downstream to supply San Francisco's water needs, we would still have two Yosemites of almost equal loveliness—can be effectively applied to other conservation situations.

Wilderness Alps of Stehekin is a 30-minute color and sound film by David Brower, including some footage by Nathan Clark, John Handley,

Charles Hessey, and Martin Litton. It tells a story of wilderness and people and of the magnificent peaks, glaciers, forests, flowers, and wildlife of the Cascades lying north of Stevens Pass, in northern Washington. Two boys and their father, having glimpsed some of the nation's greatest parklands, explore with friends the little-known mountain world at the head of Lake Chelan, "the American Alps," and discover for themselves how much this region deserves to be protected as a great primeval national park. They seek no high adventure—although this is the place for it—but keep instead to the friendly country, the forest aisles and high gardens. They find an irreplaceable part of America the beautiful, in primitive country that still has a *beyond* to it, and wildness the ages have made perfect.

"Wilderness Alps" does not try to hammer any points home. But you know that this country, and all the subtle vitalness its wilderness has, is country worth caring about and caring for.

Stehekin is a town, a river, a valley, and a way of life at the head of Lake Chelan in America's deepest canyon, dramatic gateway to the North Cascades country. Abigail Avery, her husband, Stuart, and their children —all from Lincoln, Massachusetts—know the country well from many summer visits, which resulted in her giving the club a generous grant for the film. The Conservation and Memorial Fund added to this, as did appropriations from the club general fund and proceeds from sales of copies. As a result, this is the club's most successful film venture, with fifty copies now being circulated all over the country, and being very gratifyingly praised.

Films in preparation. As this revision of the Handbook goes to press, completion is being rushed of "An Island in Time: The Point Reyes Peninsula," by Laurel Reynolds and Mindy Willis, to tell of the need for preserving a national seashore at Point Reyes and of the need for seashore preservation on all our coasts.

Professor Robert C. Stebbins, University of California zoölogist, is completing "Nature is Next Door," based on the wildlife of Tilden Regional Park, east of Berkeley, and the meaning of such places as thresholds to wilderness. Dr. Stebbins has still another film under way, aided by a grant to the club for this purpose by the Conservation Foundation—"No Room for Wilderness," based on his footage, of wildlife and people, exposed in the course of his sabbatical to South Africa in 1958–59. Walter Ward is completing a film on the club itself, portraying the club's scope and activities, primarily for showings to outsiders. Richard Bayne, of Seattle, is completing the shooting of a film of the Salmon La Sac country of Washington. And the club is distributing magnetic-sound copies of two color films on the North Cascades by Charles Hessey, of Naches, Washington—"Winter in the Cascades" and "Glacier Peak Holiday"—and of the Quetico-superior country too.

The motion-picture program has thus expanded from tentative beginnings, and has a potential that has not yet been fully explored. At this midway point, however, with 15 copies of "Two Yosemites," 21 of "Wilderness River Trail," and 50 of "Wilderness Alps" (one of them going the rounds in Thailand!) all in circulation, we are approaching the point where it may be claimed that the sun never sets on a Sierra Club film showing. The growing support of the publications program, of which the motion pictures are now part, promises early realization of this wide audience for conservation.

* * *

Slides. Color stills have their place, too, and gifts made by generous members started the Visual Education Committee on a program it had long wanted to undertake. Charles T. Townsend and Richard G. Johnson presented to the Natural Science Section of the San Francisco Bay Chapter some of their own fine 35mm. color slides. Charles S. Webber, known to many a club member for his beautiful flower photographs, has given nearly three thousand slides, including both pictures in natural color and a number of earlier hand-colored slides. It was not long before the Section realized that the scope and use of such a collection ought to be club-wide, and its Slide Committee has merged with the Visual Education Committee. The mounting and cataloguing has been completed for most of the slides so far donated, and a variety of sets of slides, together with descriptive cards, is available for loan or rent—within or outside the club—for special programs. The Visual Education Committee looks forward to a continual enlargement of the collection—through direct gift or by loan.

All films are available to schools and organizations. A small charge is collected whenever it works no hardship, in order to keep the revolving fund for motion pictures revolving.

Bequests and Gifts

THROUGH all of its early years the Sierra Club struggled with limited financial resources. Seven years after its formation the balance in its treasury was but $46.05. Not until the thirteenth year did this balance exceed $1,000. In that year, 1905, the directors wisely created a permanent fund by setting aside $100 for such fund from the club's then total net worth of $1,107. By the end of 1959 the $100 had grown to $130,000, the $1,107 to $400,000, exclusive of real property totaling about 1400 acres.

Perhaps the most important factor in its growth has been bequests and gifts from members and friends. Records now available are not so complete as to permit enumerating all the contributions received but some of them will be listed. Not all of them have been added to the Permanent Fund. Many have been used for specific purposes, in accordance with the wishes of the donors or the decisions of the Board of Directors.

The first bequest was from the world-famed English mountaineer Edward Whymper. It was received in 1911 and amounted to fifty pounds. It is altogether fitting that Edward Whymper's name should head the list, not only because his is one of the most famous names in mountaineering annals but because of his admiration for the Sierra Club. In his later life, when disposing of much of his mountaineering library, he held his set of the club's annual *Bulletins* as one of his most treasured possessions. After his death this set was secured by Aurelia S. Harwood, who willed it to William E. Colby. He later presented it to the club.

The second bequest was received in 1918 from First Lieutenant Robert S. Gillett who lost his life during World War I in an airplane accident in Texas on September 17, 1918. It amounted to $1,000. He resided in Connecticut, far from the Sierra, but he had a real love for the range. He specified that his bequest be used for the upkeep of the John Muir Trail or the upkeep of the Parsons Memorial Lodge in Tuolumne Meadows. This fund is now held in the club's endowment fund and the income derived from it is devoted to lodge maintenance.

During her lifetime the club received several generous gifts from Aurelia S. Harwood and these were supplemented in 1930 by a bequest of $1,000. In all, $5,000 of the Permanent Fund, derived from her generosity, is carried as the Aurelia S. Harwood Fund. It was her wish that the income from this fund be used, at least in large measure, for care and maintenance of Parsons and LeConte lodges. She was President of the Sierra Club, 1926-28.

In 1931 a bequest of $10,000 was received from Stephen T. Mather, first director of the National Park Service and an enthusiastic member.

In 1932 Henry H. Palmer, long a member of the club and participant in many of its annual outings left a bequest of nearly $3,500.

In 1938 a bequest of $500 was received from Alfred P. Redington to be used for something of a permanent character at Shasta Alpine Lodge.

In 1930 the construction of a shelter hut on Muir Pass was financed in the club's behalf by George Frederick Schwarz, of Brewster, Massachusetts. At the time of his death he had contributed $3,500 toward the cost of this project. After his death his estate made a further contribution of $2,300 to complete the project.

The late M. Hall McAllister for many years made generous contributions, for the construction, maintenance and operation of Shasta Alpine Lodge situated upon the club's property on the slope of Mount Shasta. He underwrote the cost of the cable on Half Dome. Owing to his modesty, the total amount of his gifts is unknown. He left a bequest of $2,500.

In 1935 John P. Dexter gave the club stock and cash amounting to $500, for the improvement of the property in Tuolumne Meadows.

The construction of the Peter Grubb Shelter in 1937 was stimulated by a gift from William Whittlesey Burd. Its enlargement to the present Peter Grubb Hut was made possible through Mr. and Mrs. D. Hanson Grubb, who have repeatedly contributed substantial sums toward the financing and upkeep of this structure, which is a memorial to their son, Peter Grubb. Many members added their contribution, as they had for Clair Tappaan Lodge.

In 1946 Mr. and Mrs. Walter A. Starr gave the club $1,000 to be used as a revolving fund to assist in defraying the cost of publishing revised editions of Starr's *Guide*. They contributed generously and frequently to this and similar projects, including the exhibit and book, *This Is the American Earth*, their gifts totaling more than $12,000 at this writing.

In 1947 Mr. and Mrs. William Shand of Lancaster, Pennsylvania, gave $3,000 to be used for a suitable memorial to their son, Dr. William Shand, Jr. This is now being used for the publication of a Climber's Guide. They also donated the mountaineering library of their son, and it is now available for reference in the rooms for the club in Los Angeles.

Securities and cash valued at approximately $23,000 came to the club in 1950 through the generosity of Ynes Mexía, world-famous botanical collector and long-time member, who set up a trust at the time of her death in 1938. The Ynes Mexía Publications Fund is due chiefly to her bequest.

Mrs. Frederick H. Morley, life member and the widow of an enthusiastic member who lost his life in an unfortunate mountaineering accident in 1921, bequeathed $20,000 to the club in 1950 with provision that income derived from this fund be used to defray expenses of certain persons not otherwise able to participate in the club's annual outings, under conditions to be determined by the directors. This fund has been increased by donations from generous club members, and each year about a dozen people are enabled to participate in the summer outings as guests. Half of these have been Americans, the rest foreign exchange students or teachers.

William E. Colby has generously presented many valuable letters of John Muir, valuable paintings, and books. It was at Colby's suggestion that a fund raised on the return from the Glacier National Park outing in 1924 was presented to the club to be used in furthering the creation of Kings Canyon National Park. This fund was placed at interest and in 1939 the accumulated total amounted to upwards of $2,000. It was used most effectively in that year for the publication of a descriptive, illustrated pamphlet setting forth the reasons for creation of this park.

The club is indebted to the late Albert Bender for gifts and bequests of money and of works of art. These also include the purchase of valuable letters written by John Muir to Robert Underwood Johnson.

In 1912, the Soda Springs property in the Tuolumne Meadows was purchased through contributions from approximately seventy members of the club in amounts of $100 or $200 each. The title to the property stands in the name of the Sierra Club but originally the donors of the purchase money reserved equitable interests. Most of these equitable interests have since been donated to the club.

The late Jesse B. Agnew in 1923 gave the club title to 80 acres of land on the floor of Kings River Canyon. This important holding embraces the westerly portion of Zumwalt Meadow and extends to Granite Creek.

Another bequest from Charles A. Cavanagh, approximating $2,000, was received in 1950. Half of this amount has been donated to the Marin Conservation League as a contribution to the Willis Linn Jepson Memorial—the preservation of an area of Bishop pines and other flora in the Tomales Bay State Park in Marin County.

A bequest of $3,000 was received from Alfred Edward Baldwin in 1951, of which one half was allocated to the Angeles Chapter. In that same year the Guymon Cabins, on Cleveland National Forest, San Diego County, were donated to the club by E. T. Guymon, Jr.

Part of John I. Miller's bequest of approximately $4,400 has been used to further the establishment of State Parks in Marin County—$1,000 for an addition to Mount Tamalpais State Park lands, and $1,875 to the Marin Conservation League for the beach park on Tomales Bay.

In 1955 William P. Young bequeathed $500 to the Sierra Club, which he had joined only a short time before his death.

The will of Marion Randall Parsons, long a member of the Editorial Board and onetime director of the club, established a substantial trust, totaling more than $43,000, which passed to the club in 1959.

The club has received a bequest exceeding $50,000, plus real property, under the will of Jean Howard McDuffie, widow of former club president Duncan McDuffie.

Early in 1956, through the generosity of members of the Sierra Ski Club, the Sierra Club acquired Hutchinson Lodge and the 67 acres of property adjoining it in the vicinity of Norden.

Subsequent to 1956 the club's properties continued to grow. The Sierra negatives of Cedric Wright were willed to the club, and Helen LeConte and Joseph LeConte donated the Sierra negatives of J. N. LeConte, early Sierra explorer and long-time Honorary President. Contributions to the Russell H. Varian Memorial Fund brought about purchase by the club of the 27-acre Castle Rock Memorial Park. Gifts from Harold Bradley and his family and friends led to the addition of the Josephine Bradley Memorial Hut on the Donner-to-Echo ski-hut chain.

Publications, studies, and photography were given major financial assistance. Abigail Avery, of Lincoln, Massachusetts, donated $2,500 toward production of "Wilderness Alps of Stehekin" (made in addition to other duties by the executive director). Max McGraw, of Dundee, Illinois, donated a total of more than $24,000 to make possible the publication of the club's first major work, *This Is the American Earth*, by Ansel Adams and Nancy Newhall, which in turn was to give a new dimension to the entire publications program. An anonymous donor gave $6,000 to assure preparation of Ansel Adams's *Portfolio III*, and of successive projects of the same photographic quality subsequent to its distribution. In June 1959 Dorothy Varian and her husband, the late Russell Varian, donated $2,500 toward the cost of conservation studies and photography in the Pacific Northwest, and later that year Dr. and Mrs. Stirling A. Colgate contributed stock valued at $2,800 to aid a continuation of those studies and publication upon them. In the course of the year Resources for the Future, itself financed by a Ford Foundation grant, contributed $2,500 to the Sixth Biennial Wilderness Conference and publication of its proceedings. In the same year the Conservation Foundation, in New York City, contributed $1,000 to help the same purpose and to further the work on the Stebbins film, "No Room for Wilderness."

Unfortunately, a complete roster of donors cannot be compiled from available records. Even if the list were complete, it would contain an enormous gap—the value of the time contributed to the club's good work by thousands of members through the sixty-eight years that have brought the club to press time for this edition of the Handbook. The club lives and breathes on three kinds of support—moral, physical, and financial. It will die if any of these three fails. But this is not likely to happen as long as love of the land still lives, and generosity, and a willingness to put dollars to work in the saving of things that dollars cannot replace.

* * *

The Conservation and Memorial Fund.—Reminded of what High Trippers had accomplished in 1924 by their contributions to a fund that helped create Kings Canyon National Park, another group of High Trippers added substantially to a Conservation and Memorial Fund in 1950, so that there would be a reserve for similar emergencies in the future. The fund itself had started quietly two years earlier, "to be drawn on for conservation work when some unusual need arises that cannot be met out of the normal budget." Gifts have come in widely varying amounts, more often than not in memory of a friend who was a member, perhaps in lieu of flowers. All told, gifts have exceeded $22,000. They have made such conservation achievements as these possible:

Photography of Dinosaur National Monument by Philip Hyde and Charles Eggert ("Wilderness River Trail"), drawn on heavily in the effort to save the monument.

The film, "Two Yosemites," inspired also by the Dinosaur campaign but of great value in any effort to keep dams out of the wrong places.

Four years of North Cascades studies and photography by David R. Simons, and major assistance in the financing of "Wilderness Alps of Stehekin."

Production of "An Island in Time: the Point Reyes Peninsula," by Laurel Reynolds and Mindy Willis.

Other films and work now in progress—all potential gains that would not have come about without the fund standing by to give support. The work of devoted members can go on, in their memory.

Folklore

THE START took place on Saturday, the 13th, at 5 a.m. Some rode horseback out of the valley, but nearly all of the party walked out over the trail. Few of us will ever forget this delightful tramp, starting as we did in the cool of the early morning, avoiding the heat of the day with its discomforts and enjoying the views of the valley as it spread out before us ... the trip was made interesting by the obstacles to be surmounted, and it was a sight to see dignified college professors, wily limbs of the law, deft doctors, and reverend clergymen join gleefully in rolling rocks, lifting logs, and shoveling snow to make way for the commissary."

Thus, in the *Sierra Club Bulletin* of January, 1902, did Edward T. Parsons write of the start of the Sierra Club's first outing, of its organized exploring and enjoying of the mountains. In the course of these outings, which have taken large parties alone into the mountains for weeks at a time, it is natural that many unique customs, traditions, and practices have grown up. Then, too, certain conditions and qualities—limited amounts of equipment and material possessions; "obstacles to be surmounted"; variety of talents and accomplishments; love of the mountains and mountain life; joy of exploring fresh new summits, trails, and wilderness country; satisfaction of gathering with friends and acquaintances around huge blazing campfires—these combined have inevitably brought forth many songs and stories, poems and jingles, plays and entertainments, expressing or suggesting the spirit and life of the outings. Many of these spontaneous expressions have been short-lived, to entertain or cheer for a moment, then vanish like the light of the campfire; while others have been passed along from one outing to another. Fortunately, some have been written down—for the most part in the Sierra Club Folklore Scrapbook compiled by Irma Weill which is in the club library. Selections from it appear in earlier editions of the Handbook, and are especially enjoyable to people who have shared the experiences of wilderness outings. More generally appreciated are some recent technical advances in mountaineering equipment. Many of these have been sketched in the course of their actual use on cliffs and ski slopes and were presented to the mountaineering world for the first time in a catalog of skiing and climbing equipment offered by the Little Gem Co., May Pridham, President. The catalog was compiled from a series of sketches appearing in *Mugelnoos,* and was published in the *Sierra Club Bulletin,* February, 1941. The catalog is reprinted in the following pages, in the belief that present members should be familiar with the devices described.

LITTLE GEM CO.
May Pridham, *President*
CLIMBING AND SKIING EQUIPMENT CATALOG

LITTLE GEM PARACHUTE

Never a dissatisfied user.
Use the Little Gem Parachute
once and you never will use
any other. It is easily fitted
to any rucksack.

CAUTION: In using the
Little Gem Parachute the
climber must not raise his
arms. However, in case
he does make this mistake,
the rucksack is still lowered
in perfect safety.

LITTLE GEM EXPOSURE COLLAR

This is a specially designed collar
for those unfortunate climbers who
are unable to stand heights. The
collar prevents the climber from
looking down, so he does not
worry about the exposure.

LITTLE GEM SUCTION CUPS

For high-angle friction climbs. With the use of the Little Gem Suction Cups even the most difficult overhangs become child's play.

CAUTION: Not suitable for use on sandstone.

LITTLE GEM ROPE NIPPERS

Ideal for use when it becomes necessary to unrope in a hurry.

SUGGESTION: When one member of a party is equipped with a pair of these nippers, it is advisable that the other members of the party equip themselves with Little Gem Parachutes.

LITTLE GEM ROPING-DOWN BAG

Provides a de-luxe method for roping-down.

CAUTION: Do not let go of the rope.
In an emergency this bag may be used as a substitute for the Little Gem Parachute.
It may also be used as a bivouac sack when fastened to a piton.

LITTLE GEM CLIMBERS' HATS

Useful as well as stylish. The ornaments are removable brushes especially designed for clearing off handholds.

LITTLE GEM ICE-AX CUSHION

Easily fastened to the head of any ice-ax. Without this cushion you do not get full value from the most common use of the ice-ax.

LITTLE GEM SAFETY BELT

This Little Gem Safety Belt adapts a new-type life preserver to the use of the skier. When the skier feels a spill coming on, a pull on the rip-cord combines two chemicals which form a gas, thus inflating the belt. After a spill, a second pull on the rip-cord deflates the belt.

CAUTION:
Deflate at once!

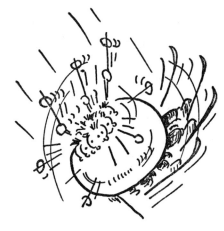

**LITTLE GEM
SKI BOOSTER**

Easily attached
to any pair of
skis. Especially adapted to
the use of the "three-track"
type of skier. The height is
adjustable and may be raised
or lowered as confidence is
gained or lost.

**LITTLE GEM
SUPER-GELANDESPRUNG SKI POLES**

The shaft of the pole is a strong
spring. Simply insert poles, exert
pressure, and take off.

NOTE: Beginners are urged not
to press too hard.

LITTLE GEM SUNBURN PREVENTER

The only sure way to prevent sunburn.
All goozles are unreliable.

CAUTION: This device is not adaptable
to the use of the rock-climber.

LITTLE GEM SPRING BELT

The belt is strapped on with the spring over the spot upon which a forced landing is most likely to be made.

In case of a fall, the victim is immediately snapped back to his previous position, no altitude being lost.

NOTE: Great care should be taken to land on the spring. Otherwise the belt is useless.

LITTLE GEM RUBBER PITONS

Guaranteed to fit any crack. As they can be pushed in with the fingers, no hammer is needed. They can be used over and over again.

CAUTION: Due to the ease with which the Little Gem Rubber Pitons are inserted, they also come out rather easily. It is best to be equipped with a Little Gem Parachute when using these pitons.

APPENDIX

A Sierra Club Chronology

1892

Sierra Club founded. Officers elected June 4, John Muir, President; Articles of Incorporation filed June 17; charter membership, 182.

Aided defeat of proposal to reduce Yosemite boundaries.

First publication issued: *Articles of Association, Articles of Incorporation, By-Laws, and List of Charter Members.*

1893

Sierra Forest Reserves, advocated by club, established.

First *Sierra Club Bulletin* issued.

Published J. N. LeConte's two maps, Yosemite, and the Kings River region, a major geographical contribution.

Room for exclusive use of club procured and furnished in Academy of Sciences Building, Market Street.

1894

John Muir recommended trail through Tuolumne Canyon.

Registers placed on six peaks, the first step in the mountain-records program that has been carried on by the club ever since.

1895

At annual meeting, Joseph LeConte, William R. Dudley and John Muir spoke on national parks and forest reservations, and urgency of preservation through national government reservation. Muir also urged recession of Yosemite Valley to federal government; Dudley, the preservation of groves of Coast redwoods.

Published *Table of Elevations within the Pacific Coast,* compiled by Mark B. Kerr and R. H. Chapman.

Theodore S. Solomons and Walter A. Starr completed the quest for a high-mountain route between Yosemite and Kings Canyon.

1896

Directors offered assistance in work of Forestry Commission, appointed by the National Academy of Sciences, in its visit to Pacific Coast.

Published map of the central portion of Sierra Nevada and of the Yosemite Valley.

1897

Sierra Point in Yosemite named by Charles A. Bailey in honor of Sierra Club.

Club urged strengthening of public forest policy and supported report of U.S. Forestry Commission (appointed by National Academy of Sciences) urging creation of additional "national forest parks" to include Grand Canyon and Mount Rainier. Membership reached 350.

1898

Sierra Club headquarters established in Yosemite Valley, with William E. Colby as custodian, to stimulate excursions and further educational work of club.

Club urged creation of parks to preserve Coast redwoods.

1899

Urged reservation of all government forest land about headwaters of Sacramento River system.

Mount Rainier National Park created by Act of Congress; bill based on memorial prepared by several organizations, including Sierra Club.

1900

Assisted in efforts to save North Grove, Calaveras Big Trees.

Joseph LeConte's *Ramblings Through the High Sierra* republished.

1901

First Sierra Club Outing arranged by John Muir as part of program to educate the people about the values of preserving mountain regions; William E. Colby, leader. Held in Yosemite Valley and Tuolumne Meadows.

San Francisco, through James D. Phelan, Mayor, applied for reservoir sites at Lake Eleanor and Hetch Hetchy. Applications denied, 1903, and 1905, by E. A. Hitchcock, Secretary of the Interior.

1902

First Kings River Outing conducted.

1903

President Theodore Roosevelt visited Yosemite and Mariposa Grove with John Muir.

First Kern River Outing conducted; first mass ascent, by outing party of about forty persons, of Mount Whitney.

LeConte Memorial Lodge, in Yosemite Valley, constructed, in memory of Joseph LeConte who died in Yosemite Valley, July 6, 1901.

Club office moved to Mills Building. Membership, 663.

Published *A Flora of the South Fork of Kings River,* prepared by Alice Eastwood.

Club published article on "How to Make 'Skis' "—7–12 feet long.

1904

Committee on Names active in interest of establishing appropriate names for mountains of California.

Local Walks inaugurated in San Francisco region.

1905

State legislature receded Yosemite Valley and Mariposa Big Tree Grove to federal government, largely through efforts of John Muir, William E. Colby, and other members of the club.

Aided in establishing State Forestry and transfer of management of federal forest reserves from Department of the Interior to Department of Agriculture.

First Washington outing conducted, to Mount Rainier (also Mount Hood and Mount Shasta).

Acting jointly with Mazamas, recommended action for betterment of Mount Rainier National Park.

By-Laws amended to authorize formation of a Southern California Section.

1906

Joint Resolution of Congress, June 11, accepted recession of Yosemite Grant.

Sent report to President of U.S., Secretary of Agriculture, and Forester, on Kings River Canyon and vicinity, to call public attention to region and induce government to make it more accessible and protect it.

Five thousand rainbow trout planted in Copper Creek and 15,000 eastern brook trout
in hitherto fishless waters of Paradise Valley, the beginning of a public benefit carried on by the club for several years.

San Francisco earthquake and fire. Club records and library destroyed.

1907

Sierra Club Committee, appointed by president, in resolution to Secretary of the
Interior, opposed use of Hetch Hetchy Valley as reservoir site.

1908

James R. Garfield, Secretary of the Interior, granted permit allowing San Francisco
to develop Lake Eleanor and Cherry Valley, and if these proved insufficient, then
Hetch Hetchy.

Collected scientific data and photographs, and published throughout nation to inform the people concerning national park values of Hetch Hetchy.

Club membership reached 1,000.

1909

Under auspices of club, trail practically completed connecting Kings Canyon with
Paradise Valley, opening up Woods Creek and Rae Lakes country.

1910

Aided in establishment of Glacier National Park, and supported other national parks.

Devil's Postpile and Rainbow Falls endangered by proposed reservoir; club urged
study and preservation as national monument.

Secretary of the Interior R. A. Ballinger required San Francisco "to show why the
Hetch Hetchy Valley and reservoir site should not be eliminated from said permit" of 1908. Board of Army Engineers appointed to investigate.

1911

Devil's Postpile National Monument established through work of Walter Huber.

Favored enlargement of Sequoia National Park to include Kern High Sierra.

Southern California (Angeles) Chapter organized on permanent and active basis.

1912

Urged establishment of a national park service.

Soda Springs property in Tuolumne Meadows acquired by club to preserve against
development harmful to the park.

1913

Hetch Hetchy fight lost with passage of Raker Bill.

Southern California Chapter completed Muir Lodge, in the Sierra Madre.

First organized snow trip, to Truckee, conducted.

1914

Aided in inauguration of Yosemite natural history survey under Joseph Grinnell and
Tracy I. Storer, outstanding University of California scientists.

Sierra Club Outing included, for the last time, Hetch Hetchy Valley.

John Muir died, December 24.

1915
Members of the club secured passage of bill in state legislature appropriating $10,000 for construction of John Muir Trail, the first of five such appropriations (1917, 1925, 1927, 1929).

Parsons Memorial Lodge, in Tuolumne Meadows, constructed.

1916
Supported bill which created National Park Service, whose "fundamental purpose," phrased in the law by Frederick Law Olmsted, Jr., "is to conserve the scenery and the natural and historic objects and the wild life [in the parks and monuments] and to provide for the enjoyment of the same in such manner and by such means as will leave them unimpaired for the enjoyment of future generations."

1917
Protested grazing in national parks as unnecessary wartime measure.

More than 50 members in active service (World War I).

1918
Urged enlargement of Sequoia National Park to include headwaters of Kings and Kern rivers.

About 140 members in service.

1919
Supported Save-the-Redwoods League and protested threats to redwoods.

Continued work in interest of legislation to enlarge Sequoia National Park.

Publicized dangers of sheep grazing on west slope of Sierra.

Cable-stairway placed on Half Dome, under auspices of club, by gift of M. Hall McAllister.

LeConte Memorial Lodge removed from vicinity of Camp Curry and reconstructed on present site.

1920
Supported Greater Sequoia Park in national campaign, with Marion R. Parsons representing club in East.

National Parks excluded from jurisdiction of Federal Power Commission.

Opposed proposal for major dams in Yellowstone National Park.

1921
Active in support of Sequoia National Park enlargement bill, with Francis P. Farquhar as representative of the club in East and in Washington.

Favored purchase of redwoods in Humboldt County as a State Park.

Trail connecting Yosemite Valley and northern Yosemite National Park, urged by club, partially completed.

1922
Continued campaign to enlarge Sequoia National Park.

Shasta Alpine Lodge constructed.

1923
Continued work for enlargement of Sequoia National Park.

Water Power filings on valleys of Kings River region denied by Federal Power Commission, owing in part to effective club representation.

Aided Stephen T. Mather in purchase of Redwood Meadow tract, near Giant Forest, for presentation to government when Sequoia National Park enlarged.

Zumwalt Meadow land in Kings Canyon presented to club by the late Jesse B. Agnew.
Board of Directors increased from 9 to 15 members.
First bimonthly *Sierra Club Circular* published.

1924

Continued activities for Sequoia enlargement; William E. Colby represented the club in Washington.
Advocated legislation to create State Park Commission and to make statewide survey of lands suitable for state park purposes, under leadership of Duncan McDuffie.
San Francisco Bay Chapter organized.

1925

Renewed activity in Sequoia National Park enlargement.
Trail completed down Tuolumne Canyon from Waterwheel Falls to Pate Valley, as first recommended by John Muir and urged by club.
Contributed to nature-guide work in Tuolumne Meadows under auspices of NPS.
Inaugurated new plan of educational work in gathering collection of mountain photographs to be loaned for exhibit to educational and other institutions.

1926

Sequoia National Park enlarged to include Kern and Kaweah sections and Mount Whitney.
Joined other organizations in successfully opposing Stanfield Grazing Bill, a threat to good administration of lands under Forest Service.
Published *Place Names of the High Sierra* by Francis P. Farquhar.

1927

California State Park Commission established by Legislature; William E. Colby its first chairman.
Supported Calaveras Grove Association and Save-the-Redwoods League in efforts to save Calaveras Big Trees.
Urged Forest Service to eliminate sheep grazing from Mount Ritter-Devils Postpile region.

1928

State Park Bonds authorized.
Urged acquisition of private lands in national parks by congressional appropriation matched by private subscriptions.
Sierra Club Circular became bimonthly *Bulletin*.
Contributed $1,000 to Park Service to purchase Camp Lewis in Sequoia National Park.

1929

Coöperated with outdoor and conservation organizations in San Francisco Bay area to secure establishment of Tamalpais State Park.
William E. Colby retired as manager of Outings after twenty-ninth Outing, but remained Chairman of Outing Committee.

1930

Muir Pass Shelter Hut built, through gifts from G. Frederick Schwarz.
Harwood Memorial Lodge constructed.
Published new edition of *Ramblings Through the High Sierra* by Joseph LeConte.

1931

Use of rope and sound belaying in rock climbing introduced to club by Francis P. Farquhar (N. face of Unicorn) and Robert L. M. Underhill (E. face of Banner) in course of club outing. Followed by first ascents of routes on North Palisade, Thunderbolt Peak, and E. face of Whitney.

Two Sierra Club parties swam through Muir Gorge.

1932

Urged NPS to investigate Admiralty Island (Alaska) as national park for preserving wildlife.

Riverside Chapter established.

Club headquarters moved to 1050 Mills Tower.

Organized local rock climbing practice initiated in Sierra Club by Richard M. Leonard.

Winter Sports Committee organized.

Federation of Western Outdoor Clubs organized at Mt. Hood Convention.

1933

Advised on Park Service plans for realignment of Tioga Road.

Loma Prieta Chapter organized.

1934

Joined Federation of Western Outdoor Clubs.

Clair Tappaan Lodge at Norden constructed.

Published *Guide to the John Muir Trail* by Walter A. Starr, Jr.

First ascents of Higher and Lower Cathedral Spires made by club parties.

1935

Opposed building of another road into Kings River Canyon.

Favored legislation to create Olympic National Park and urged passage of bill to create Kings Canyon National Park.

Recommended that boundaries of Death Valley National Monument be extended to include portion of west slopes of Panamint Range, chiefly for conserving wildlife.

San Antonio Hut built.

1936

Endorsed general features of Forest Service master plan for Kings River Canyon, while continuing to advocate preservation of region as national park, with Ansel Adams representing club in East.

Urged that Department of the Interior maintain high national-park standards, and suggested that a division of the National Park Service be set up to concern itself with the great primeval parks alone.

San Antonio Hut burned, was rebuilt.

1937

Supported legislation to add Carl Inn sugar pine tract to Yosemite National Park.

Opposed water-diversion tunnel under Rocky Mountain National Park.

Peter Grubb Shelter and White Rock Lake Hut constructed.

1938

Studied details of proposed Kings Canyon National Park. Club President Joel H. Hildebrand accompanied party surveying area to be included.

Conferred with Regional Forester and staff on High Sierra primitive area policies.

Protested proposal to dam Yellowstone Lake.

Dinosaur National Monument enlarged.

Section of John Muir Trail over Mather Pass constructed, thus completing the trail as originally conceived.

First club Burro and Knapsack trips conducted.

Keller Peak Ski Hut built and Peter Grubb Memorial Hut completed.

1939

Campaigned for bill to establish Kings Canyon National Park; published and distributed booklet to support Gearhart Bill; enlisted support of many national conservation groups that were at first adamant toward park; filmed *Sky-Land Trails of the Kings.*

Club represented at National Park Superintendents' 5-day Conference at Santa Fe, N. M., by Richard M. Leonard.

Favored inclusion of Butano redwoods in state park system.

Mother Lode Chapter authorized (organization meeting, January 1940).

First club Saddle Horse Trip conducted.

Shiprock, in New Mexico, climbed by club party.

1940

Kings Canyon National Park established by Congress.

Opposed authorizing sale of state parks if legislature found them more valuable for oil and gas than for recreation.

Opposed bill to authorize the President temporarily to transfer jurisdiction over certain national forest and national park lands to War or Navy departments.

Opposed bills to open up certain national monuments to mining.

First club Base Camp Trip conducted.

1941

Opposed Winter Park Authority bill endangering the wilderness area of San Jacinto State Park.

Coöperated with California Roadside Council in endeavor to improve roadsides and regulate billboards.

Aided enlargement of Anza State Park.

Skis to the Sky-Land filmed by club, to encourage ski mountaineering.

1942

Contributed $2,500 toward acquisition by Park Service of Powers property on Lake Tenaya in Yosemite National Park.

Fiftieth anniversary of club; Articles of Incorporation amended to authorize "perpetual existence."

Manual of Ski Mountaineering, edited by David R. Brower, published as an aid to training of U.S. mountain troops.

1943

Jackson Hole National Monument successfully defended.

Echo Park dam site in Dinosaur National Monument explored by Bureau of Reclamation.

Opposed repeal of Antiquities Act (National Monuments).

Favored maintenance so far as possible of national park trails during war emergency.

Approximately 600 members in armed forces. Club harvest camps established. Club outings temporarily discontinued.

1944

Favored establishing rule that certain state parks not be used by motion picture companies.

Kearsarge Pass road disapproved.

Favored preservation of South Calaveras Grove of Big Trees.

1945

Contributed to National Tribute Grove fund in honor of members serving in armed forces in World War II.

Unsuccessfully opposed enabling bill for San Jacinto tramway.

Favored establishment of Robert Louis Stevenson State Park, Napa County.

More than 1,000 members in armed forces.

1946

Collaborated with National Park Service and Frederick Law Olmsted on landscape planning in South Fork Canyon, Kings Canyon National Park.

Opposed use of Point Lobos State Park as commercial motion picture set.

Urged State Park Commission to enforce restrictions to prevent overdevelopment of facilities connected with San Jacinto tramway.

Supported legislation in interest of Joshua Tree National Monument.

William E. Colby retired as secretary of club after serving 44 years (plus two as president).

Lost Arrow, in Yosemite Valley, climbed by club party.

Flora and Azalea Lakes purchased by club for $5,000 to protect as only remaining natural area near Donner Pass on U.S. 40.

1947

Campaigned for preservation of San Gorgonio Primitive Area, Olympic National Park, and Jackson Hole National Monument.

Natural Resources Council of America organized at Mammoth Caves National Park, to promote scientific and educational work in conservation; composed of 23 leading national conservation organizations; Sierra Club a charter member, represented by Dorothy Hill.

San Gorgonio Primitive Area retained by Chief of Forest Service after contested public hearing; club represented by Richard M. Leonard.

Opposed attempt by livestock men to hamper Forest Service control of grazing lands.

Favored preservation of Butano Forest as state park.

Sierra Club Bulletin changed from bimonthly to monthly.

Published first edition of *The Sierra Club: A Handbook*.

1948

Opposed construction of Glacier View Dam in Glacier National Park.

Urged preservation of Jackson Hole National Monument.

Protested proposed damming of Lake Solitude, Wyoming.

Kings Canyon National Park threatened by City of Los Angeles through filings for water and power development; club filed briefs in protest before Federal Power Commission, which again rejected the applications.

Formulated statement on wilderness policy in response to a request from Legislative Reference Service, Library of Congress.

San Diego Chapter established.

Club offices in San Francisco expanded.

1949

Glacier View Dam proposal, to flood 20,000 acres of Glacier National Park, rejected after public hearing, by agreement of Secretaries of Interior and Army; club represented by Olaus Murie.

Lake Solitude in Cloud Peak Wild Area, Wyoming, preserved by Secretary of Interior after public hearing attended by many national conservation organizations.

Campaigned for preservation of South Calaveras Grove and Butano Forest.

First High Sierra Wilderness Conference called; sponsored and arranged by club.

Benson Memorial Ski Hut on Mount Anderson completed by investment of $8,500 of club funds and labor, as a public service hut open to use of any ski mountaineering parties of the general public.

Published *A Climber's Guide to the High Sierra, Preliminary Edition.*

1950

Rogue River victory through order of Secretary of Interior requiring study of alternative plans and five-year study of fish and wildlife.

Grand Teton National Park enlarged to include area of former Jackson Hole National Monument, rewarding long battle by club in defense of monument.

San Jacinto tramway permit rejected by Secretary of Interior on advice of Bureau of Land Management, sustaining brief of Sierra Club and reversing Department of Agriculture.

Published *John Muir's Studies in the Sierra,* with introduction by William E. Colby.

Sierra Club Bulletin, volumes 1–5 (1892–1905) re-issued.

Joseph Nisbet LeConte, Honorary President, died February 1.

Atlantic chapter established, comprising members in New York, New Jersey, Connecticut, and Pennsylvania.

Mrs. Evelyn Todd Davies Morley bequeathed $20,000 to provide educational fund for trips in mountain areas by students and teachers.

Aided posthumous completion of François E. Matthes' geological studies in Sierra.

Castle Rock Spire and north face of Sentinel Rock climbed by club parties.

1951

Dinosaur National Monument dam controversy covered in detail in special issue of *Sierra Club Bulletin.*

Continued opposition to San Jacinto tramway.

Sponsored Second Biennial Wilderness Conference.

Published *Going Light—With Backpack or Burro,* edited by David R. Brower.

Guymon cabins in Cleveland National Forest, San Diego County, donated to club by E. T. Guymon, Jr.

Tomales Bay State Park acquisition completed after contribution of $1,875 of club funds and loan of equal amount to Marin Conservation League.

Bureau of Reclamation barred by order of Secretary of Interior from surveys and investigations within national parks, national monuments, or established wilderness areas or wildlife refuges.

1952

Dinosaur National Monument protected temporarily by action of Secretary of Interior Oscar L. Chapman in ordering further study of alternate dam sites.

Clean Camp campaign inaugurated as educational program to eliminate litter.

Los Padres and Kern-Kaweah chapters established.

David R. Brower became first Executive Director of club.

California Himalayan Committee's plans for scientific work and exploration near Mt. Everest endorsed by club.

Published *Fifty-Seven-Year Index, Sierra Club Bulletin,* compiled by George Shochat and Dorothy H. Bradley.

First Family Burro Trip held as part of summer outings.

Kings Canyon National Park threatened by renewal of Los Angeles 1920 and 1948 applications for water and power developments. Sierra Club protested.

Gila Wilderness Area in New Mexico established by Secretary of Agriculture after public hearing before Forest Service, Weldon F. Heald representing club.

1953

Olympic National Park completed; President Truman added 47,000 acres to Park.

Butano Forest acquisition aided by $6,000 contribution to State Park Commission by club and its members.

Sponsored Third Biennial Wilderness Conference.

Tehipite Chapter established.

Name of Southern California Chapter changed to Angeles Chapter.

First River Trips held as part of summer outings. More than 200 members took 6-day exploratory trip down the Yampa and Green rivers, Dinosaur National Monument.

Wilderness River Trail produced and widely shown by the club as 28-minute Kodachrome sound film displaying park values of Dinosaur National Monument.

Club represented at Mid-Century Conference on Resources for the Future at Washington, D.C.

Redwood Highway protected against logging and defacement through strenuous educational efforts of club and State Park Commission.

Tamalpais State Park enlarged with contribution of $1,000 of club funds through Miller bequest.

1954

Dinosaur National Monument dams recommended by Secretary of Interior Douglas McKay, precipitating the greatest conservation battle since creation of National Park Service. Club took major part in defense of monument.

A Club River Touring Committee was organized to coördinate the growing participation in boating by members and to improve safety techniques.

California Himalayan Committee expedition to Makalu, world's fourth highest peak; substantial backing of National Science Foundation, and over $8,000 in contributions from club members.

Pacific Northwest Chapter formed.

Climber's Guide to the High Sierra, edited by Hervey Voge, published by the club.

Calaveras South Grove acquisition completed after 50 years of club effort, final action largely through persistence of Honorary Vice Presidents Albright, Drury, and Olmsted, and gift of $1,000,000 by John D. Rockefeller, Jr.

Olympic National Park boundaries again re-examined by special committee appointed by Governor Arthur Langlie of Washington; Sierra Club member Pauline Dyer was committee secretary. Governor decided not to recommend reduction.

Outing program under Chairman H. Stewart Kimball provided 24 trips in seven states to spread knowledge of outstanding scenic and wilderness areas.

Mount Rainier tramway plan defeated.

1955

Dinosaur controversy continues. Executive Director represented club at principal hearings.

Fragment of Butano Forest saved.

"This Is the American Earth," the club's most comprehensive exhibit, completed by Ansel Adams and Nancy Newhall through the generosity of Walter Starr, to become permanent display at California Academy of Sciences and LeConte Lodge; duplicates circulated by Smithsonian Institution and U.S. Information Agency.

Fourth Biennial Wilderness Conference held in Berkeley.

Club's executive director named chairman, Natural Resources Council of America.

Two Yosemites, in color and sound, was produced to apply lessons of Hetch Hetchy tragedy to Dinosaur controversy.

1956

Dinosaur controversy concluded with victory for park-preservation forces. Executive Director given National Parks Association Award in recognition of club's role. Club supported creation of Dinosaur National Park. Proposal of National Wilderness Preservation System given enthusiastic club support.

Scenic Resources Review proposed by Board of Directors.

Sierra Club Council created by vote of membership, primarily to assist with internal affairs.

Club membership reached 10,000. 1700 members participated in the 27 wilderness outings.

The club published *A Climber's Guide to the Teton Range* and *Belaying the Leader: An Omnibus on Climbing Safety.*

Major support was given to creation of a National Wilderness Preservation System.

First outings conducted to the North Cascades of Washington to help inform members and public of wilderness values involved.

1957

Toiyabe Chapter (centering in Reno) established.

First all-club Information and Education Conference held in San Francisco.

Fifth Wilderness Conference held in San Francisco on theme, "Wildlands in Our Civilization," with participation by chiefs of principal wilderness-administering agencies.

A series of studies of the public values of the North Cascades Region was initiated and the filming was completed of the club's second major production, *Wilderness Alps of Stehekin.*

1958

The second club-wide Information and Education Conference was held in San Francisco.

The club conducted its first outing to the Wind River Mountains of Wyoming to build support for the high-caliber wilderness of the region.

The Redwood Chapter was formed.

1959

The Sixth Biennial Wilderness Conference was held in San Francisco on the theme, "The Meaning of Wilderness to Science," with financial assistance from Resources for the Future and the Conservation Foundation and an international representation of scientists.

The final effort was begun to transform into book form the club's major exhibit, "This Is the American Earth," and was greatly assisted by a grant of $15,000 from the McGraw Foundation.

The monthly *Sierra Club Bulletin* format was enlarged.

The Great Lakes Chapter was established.

Virginia Ferguson retired as Assistant Secretary after 32 years' service.

1960

Club membership reached 15,000.

This Is the American Earth, by Ansel Adams and Nancy Newhall, was published as the first major club book, and as a direct result a major expansion in the club's conservation-publishing program was begun.

Sierra Club Membership, 1892-1960

Ski and Climbing Tests

THE SIERRA CLUB tests were adapted from those designed by the Ski Club of Great Britain and accepted and revised by the National Ski Association. The club tests contain a few additional requirements giving greater emphasis to touring.

When a skier feels reasonably able to pass a test, he should get in touch with one of the judges as listed from season to season in the *Bulletin* and posted on ski-lodge bulletin boards. The current test requirements are available at the club's lodges. The purposes of each test follow.

4th class: To determine the candidate's competence to engage in easy cross-country ski trips. Good form is desirable but will not be insisted upon.

3d class: To stimulate and measure the ordinary touring ability every skier should be ambitious to attain in order to enjoy all-day tours over mountain terrain. Fluency, assurance, steadiness are required rather than speed.

2d class: To demonstrate mastery of touring technique and ability to cope with all conditions of snow and terrain, including steep slopes and open woods, that are not unjustifiably hazardous. Marked steadiness and a fluent style are required. The speed expected is approximately double that for Third Class, but not necessarily more than half that of racing speed. No kick-turns are permitted in any part of this test. Few falls are allowed.

The First Class award is made for excellence in either touring or racing:

The *touring* award is intended as a recognition of perfected technique and notable performance, including leadership, in ski mountaineering and touring. No person shall be eligible unless he has passed the ski-mountaineering test.

The *racing* award is intended as a recognition of consistently notable performance in representative and officially recognized national or international competition.

THE SIERRA CLUB SKI-MOUNTAINEERING TEST

The High Sierra may be safely toured in winter if skiers are thoroughly capable of coping with situations that may arise. The preceding tests, designed to determine cross-country skiing ability, do not attempt to cover those broader phases of winter snowcraft necessary if one is to wander from winter sports centers and marked ski trails. To measure this comprehensive ability, and to encourage skiers to acquire it, the Winter Sports Committee established the Ski-Mountaineering Test and later prepared a textbook for it, the *Manual of Ski Mountaineering,* published under the auspices of the National Ski Association, and on sale at the club offices.

The candidate, in addition to being a member of the Sierra Club who has demonstrated his interest in the club's winter trail and lodge system (this being required only for the Sierra Club Award), must satisfy the judges that he has:

1. Passed the Third Class Test.

2. Ability to use properly a topographic map and compass.

3. Knowledge of first aid and rescue technique, including the treatment of freezing and the ability to construct and use a two-ski rescue sled.

4. Knowledge of the basic principles of snowcraft, with special reference to avalanches.

5. Toured on skis two full days during the winter season, with at least one overnight camp on snow, carrying an appropriate share of total equipment during the entire tour.

6. Knowledge and demonstrated ability to use equipment necessary for safely undertaking a ski tour of several days' duration.

7. Completed the ascent and descent on skis of approximately 1,500 feet of elevation, preferably on a peak, demonstrating a knowledge of proper equipment.

8. Demonstrated ability on tour to cope with an average variety of snow conditions.

SKI PINS

The Sierra Club ski test pins and patches are available to club members in good standing upon presentation of duly signed test certificate at the Sierra Club offices. The colors on the pins are: First Class, silver; Second Class, yellow; Third Class, red; Fourth Class, green. They may also be obtained at Tappaan Lodge. The price per pin and per patch is $1.00. Arcs in color corresponding to class are available to go below patch at 25 cents each. There is no charge for the First Class award.

MEMBERSHIP TEST FOR ROCK CLIMBING SECTIONS

SINCE rock climbing is a specialized and potentially hazardous sport, the rock climbing sections of the various chapters require successful completion of a test before an individual becomes a full-fledged member of the section. Persons who have not passed the test are welcome to visit most climbs for observation and instruction. An exception is made for climbs in Yosemite Valley and certain high mountain regions, where attendance is restricted to section members.

Below is outlined the membership test of the Rock Climbing Section of the San Francisco Bay Chapter of the Sierra Club. This test is similar, but not identical, to those of other sections. Sierra Club members who wish to become section members must complete the following requirements to the satisfaction of one or more incumbent members of the Rock Climbing Committee of the section.

1. Be familiar with and demonstrate a willingness to comply with the rules on safety as set up by the section.

2. Demonstrate a knowledge of uses, and show ability to tie, the following knots: bowline, Prusik, butterfly, bowline-on-a-coil, and two knots for joining the ends of two ropes (not square knot).

3. Demonstrate a thorough knowledge of the verbal climbing signals.

4. Demonstrate ability to rappel smoothly over varying angles and heights. With coiled ropes, set up a belayed rappel, rappel down, retrieve the rappel rope, and then recoil both ropes.

5. Demonstrate ability to hold safely both lower and upper belay falls, and to rig satisfactory anchors for several belay positions, including both lower and upper belay positions.

6. Demonstrate a knowledge of the Prusik technique and its uses.

7. Demonstrate a knowledge of the rules for the care of the rope.

8. Attend a minimum of five scheduled climbs within a period of three months prior to the test. The candidate must participate in belay and rappel practice at each of these climbs, and must participate in at least one multi-pitch climb.

List of Outings

1901. Yosemite Valley and Tuolumne Meadows.
1902. Kings River Canyon and Mount Brewer.
1903. Kern River region and Mount Whitney.
1904. Yosemite National Park.
1905. Mount Rainier, Mount Hood, and Mount Shasta.
1906. Kings River region.
1907. Yosemite National Park and Mount Ritter.
1908. Kern River region and Mount Whitney.
1909. Yosemite National Park and Mount Ritter.
1910. Kings River region.
1911. Yosemite National Park.
1912. Kern River region and Cottonwood Lakes.
1913. South and Middle forks of Kings River.
1914. Yosemite National Park and Mount Ritter.
1915. Yosemite National Park and Devil's Postpile.
1916. Kern Canyon, Junction Pass, Bubbs Creek and Kearsarge Pass.
1917. Yosemite National Park.
1919. Yosemite National Park and Mount Ritter.
1920. South Fork of the San Joaquin, Middle Fork of the Kings.
1921. Yosemite National Park and Mount Ritter.
1922. Kern Canyon, Junction Pass, Kings River Canyon, Giant Forest.
1923. Yosemite National Park.
1924. Glacier National Park, Montana.
1925. South and Middle forks of Kings, South Fork of San Joaquin.
1926. Yellowstone National Park, Wyoming.
1927. Redwood Meadow, Mount Whitney, Milestone, Giant Forest.
1928. Jasper and Mount Robson parks, Canada.
1929. John Muir Trail: Blaney Meadows north to Cold Canyon.
1930. Mono, Selden, Muir passes, Palisades, Bishop Pass.
1931. Northern and eastern Yosemite National Park.
1932. Giant Forest, Sphinx Creek, Mount Whitney, Chagoopa Plateau.
1933. Piute Pass, Evolution and Palisades region, Bishop Pass.
1934. Northern Yosemite National Park.
1935. Big Meadow, Cartridge Creek, Vidette and Scaffold meadows.
1936. Giant Forest, Moraine Lake, Mount Whitney, Milestone.
1937. Glacier National Park, Montana.
1938. *High Trip:* Agnew Meadow, Banner-and-Ritter to Pine Creek Pass. *Burro Trip:* Kings River region, from Horse Corral Meadow. *Knapsack Trip:* Evolution and Palisades region.
1939. *High Trip:* Piute Pass, Evolution and Palisades, Bench Lake, Sawmill Pass. *Burro Trip:* North and south from Tuolumne Meadows. *Knapsack Trip:* Kearsarge Pass to Barnard and Williamson and Shepherd Pass. *Saddle Trip:* Sawmill Pass to Army Pass.

1940. *High Trip:* Cedar Grove, Woods Creek, Foresters Pass, Colby Pass. *Burro Trip:* San Joaquin High Sierra, from Florence Lake. *Knapsack Trip:* Palisades region. *Saddle Trip:* Over Kearsarge, Granite, Muir and Piute passes. *Base Camp:* East Lake.

1941. *High Trip:* Northern Yosemite National Park. *Burro Trip:* Bubbs Creek, Rae Lakes, Woods Creek region. *Knapsack Trip:* North Lake, Evolution region, South Lake. *Saddle Trip:* Tuolumne Meadows to Mono Pass (Mono Creek). *Base Camp:* Garnet Lake.

1946. *High Trip:* Cottonwood Pass, Mount Whitney, Palisades and Evolution region, Piute Pass. *Burro Trip:* From Tuolumne Meadows. *Knapsack Trip:* Kings-Kern Divide region; Teton National Park. *Saddle Trip:* Lower Kern country to Rock Creek and Mount Whitney. *Base Camp:* Fourth Mono Recess.

1947. *High Trip:* Agnew Meadow and Banner-and-Ritter to Pine Creek Pass. *Burro Trip:* Kings River region, from Onion Valley. *Knapsack Trip:* Evolution Group, Wind River Range, Wyoming. *Base Camp:* Fifth Lake, Big Pine Lakes Basin, below North Palisade.

1948. *High Trip:* Kings River region, north and south from Zumwalt Meadow. *Burro Trip:* From North Lake. *Knapsack Trip:* Cathedral Range and Banner-Ritter-Minarets area; Olympic National Park. *Saddle Trip:* Kearsarge Pass to Mount Whitney and Whitney Portal. *Base Camp:* Meadows, foot of East Vidette.

1949. *High Trip:* Mineral King, Hamilton Lakes, Rattlesnake Creek, Moraine Lake, Sawtooth Pass. *Burro Trip:* From Rock Creek (near Bishop). *Knapsack Trip:* From Mammoth Lakes to North Lake; Teton National Park. *Saddle Trip:* Carroll Creek to Kearsarge Pass. *Base Camp:* Rock Creek (Mitre Basin).

1950. *High Trip:* Northern Yosemite National Park, and Banner and Ritter country. *Burro Trip:* From Tuolumne Meadows, over Donohue, Agnew, Koip, and Parker passes. *Knapsack Trip:* South Lake, Palisades and Evolution country, North Lake; Glacier National Park. *Base Camp:* Middle Fork of Bishop Creek.

1951. *High Trip:* Cascade Valley, The Recesses, Seven Gables, Hutchinson Meadow, Evolution country, Palisades. *Burro Trip:* Sawmill Pass to Bishop Pass. *Knapsack Trip:* Giant Forest to Cedar Grove: Loop trip near Lake Chelan, Washington. *Saddle Trip:* Whitney Portal to Army Pass. *Base Camp:* East face of Ritter-Banner-Minaret range.

1952. *High Trip:* Kearsarge Pass, Sixty Lakes Basin, Bench Lake, Upper Basin, Palisades. *Burro Trip:* Army Pass, Milestone, Whitney Pass. *Knapsack Trip:* Circle trip from Cedar Grove. *Saddle Trip:* From Carroll Creek. *Base Camp:* Evolution Basin. *Family Burro Trip:* Young Lake, McCabe Lake, Ten Lakes.

1953. *High Trip:* Miter Basin, Crabtree Meadows, Mount Whitney, Milestone Bench, Center Basin. *Burro Trip:* Over Piute, Muir, and Bishop passes. *Knapsack Trip:* Slide Canyon, Matterhorn Peak, Mount Conness; Needle Mountains of southern Colorado; Trinity Alps. *Base Camp:* Second Mono Recess. *River Trip:* Down Yampa and Green rivers through Dinosaur National Monument.

1954. *High Trip:* Lost Canyon, Big Five Lakes, Nine Lakes, Moraine Lake, Little Five Lakes; Teton and Glacier national parks. *Burro Trip:* Kearsarge Pass, Bubbs Creek, East Lake, Sixty Lakes Basin. *Knapsack Trip:* Trinity Alps; from Mineral King; North Fork of Kings River; Yosemite, from Tuolumne

Meadows; Wind River Wilderness Area, Wyoming. *Base Camp:* Bear Creek: Three Sisters Wilderness Area, Oregon; Crabtree Creek. *Family Burro Trip:* Tuolumne Meadows, Cathedral Lake. *River Trip:* Down Yampa and Green rivers.

1955. *High Trip:* Virginia Canyon to Buckeye Creek by way of Benson Lake and back via Matterhorn Canyon, Grand Teton and Glacier national parks. *Burro Trip:* Between Piute and Mono passes. *Knapsack Trip:* Kings Canyon, Marble Mountains, North Cascades, Mount Whitney, Mount Waddington, Yosemite. *Base Camps:* Minaret Lake, Kern Basin, Mount Rainier. *Family Burro Trip:* Kings Canyon. *River Trips:* Dinosaur, Glen Canyon.

1956. *High Trip:* Carroll Creek to Whitney Portal; a circle from Whitney Portal, including Milestone Bench. Grand Teton National Park. Glacier Peak Limited Area. *Burro Trip:* Yosemite. *Knapsack Trip:* Yosemite, Trinity Alps, Palisades, Glacier Peak, Mount St. Elias region. *Base Camps:* Emerald Lake, Bench Lake, Lyman Lake (Washington). *Family Burro Trip:* Kings Canyon. *River Trips:* Dinosaur and Glen Canyon.

1957. *High Trips:* Piute Pass to South Lake by way of Muir and Bishop passes; South Lake to Taboose Pass by way of Mather Pass and Bench Lake. Glacier National Park. Grand Teton National Park. *Base Camps:* Iron Mountain, Monarch Divide, Stehekin Valley, Selkirk Range. *River Trips:* Dinosaur Trips, Glen Canyon. *Knapsack Trips:* North Fork San Joaquin, Marble Mountains, Mono Recesses, Cathedral Range, Three Sisters, Wallowas, North Fork Kings River. *Burro Trips:* Loop trips from Mineral King and Mineral King to Giant Forest. *Family Burro:* Kearsarge Pass to Taboose.

1958. *High Trips:* Pine Creek to Little Lakes Valley via Selden Pass; Little Lakes Valley to McGee Creek via Mono and McGee passes. Wind River Range. *High-light Trip:* Goddard Canyon and Blackcap Basin. *Special:* Stehekin Valley, Washington. *Base Camps:* Lamarck Lake. *Knapsack Trips:* Golden Trout Creek; North Fork Kings River; headwarters of Kern River; Salmon La Sac, Washington; Northern Yosemite; Wind River Range, Wyoming; Deadman Canyon; Mono Creek. *Burro Trips:* S. Fork San Joaquin River and Mono Recesses. *Family Burro:* South Lake to Taboose Pass. *Expedition:* Cordillera Blanca, Peru. *Clean-Up Work Party:* Kearsarge Pass. *River Trips:* Dinosaur, Glen Canyon, Salmon River.

1959. *High Trips:* Wolverton to Cedar Grove; loop trip through Rae Lakes. Wind River Range. *High-Light:* North Yosemite from Hetch Hetchy. *Back Country:* Evolution Valley. *Base Camps:* Piute Creek. Stehekin Valley. *Knapsack Trips:* Silver Divide. Kern-Kaweah, Trinity Alps, Cathedral Range, Wind Rivers, Humphreys Basin. *River Trips:* Glen Canyon, Dinosaur, Rogue River, Clearwater River. *Burro Trips:* Kearsarge Pass to Taboose Pass. *Family Burro:* South Lake to Taboose Pass. *Clean-Up Work Party:* Sabrina Basin. *Expedition:* Mount Waddington. *Special:* Glacier Peak from Lake Chelan.

Directors, Chairmen, and Honorary Members

Prepared from the secretary's records and the *Sierra Club Bulletin*. Early records were destroyed in 1906.

PRESIDENT

John Muir	1892-1914	Joel H. Hildebrand	1937-1940
Joseph N. LeConte	1915-1917	Francis D. Tappaan	1940-1941
William E. Colby	1917-1919	Walter A. Starr	1941-1943
William F. Badè	1919-1922	Duncan McDuffie	1943-1946
Clair S. Tappaan	1922-1924	Bestor Robinson	1946-1948
Robert M. Price	1924-1925	Francis P. Farquhar	1948-1949
Walter L. Huber	1925-1927	Lewis F. Clark	1949–1951
Aurelia S. Harwood	1927-1928	Harold E. Crowe	1951–1953
Duncan McDuffie	1928-1931	Richard M. Leonard	1953–1955
Phil S. Bernays	1931-1933	Alexander Hildebrand	1955–1957
Francis P. Farquhar	1933-1935	Harold C. Bradley	1957–1959
Ernest Dawson	1935-1937	Nathan C. Clark	1959–

VICE-PRESIDENT

Warren Olney }		Joel H. Hildebrand	1936-1937
J. C. Branner } 1892-1898*		Francis D. Tappaan	1937-1940
Joseph LeConte }		Walter A. Starr	1940-1941
Warren Olney	1898-1899	Bestor Robinson	1941-1943
Elliott McAllister	1899-1904	E. Stanley Jones	1943-1946
Alexander C. McAdie	1904-1913	Phil S. Bernays	1946-1948
Vernon L. Kellogg	1914-1920	Lewis F. Clark	1948-1949
Clair S. Tappaan	1920-1922	Harold E. Crowe	1949–1951
Walter L. Huber	1922-1925	Lewis F. Clark	1951–1953
Aurelia S. Harwood	1925-1927	Harold E. Crowe	1953–1954
William H. Wright	1927-1928	Alexander Hildebrand	1954–1955
Duncan McDuffie	1928	Bestor Robinson	1955–1956
Phil S. Bernays	1928-1931	A. Starker Leopold	1956–1957
Francis P. Farquhar	1931-1933	Nathan C. Clark	1957–1959
Ernest Dawson	1933-1935	Edgar Wayburn	1959–
Walter L. Huber	1935-1936		

SECRETARY

J. H. Senger (corresponding)	1892–1898	William E. Colby	1905-1917
William D. Armes (recording)	1892–1893	Joseph N. LeConte	1917-1919
Elliott McAllister (recording)	1893–1898	William E. Colby	1919-1946
W. R. Dudley (corresponding)	1898–1905	Richard M. Leonard	1946–1953
Robert M. Price (recording)	1898–1900	Lewis F. Clark	1953–1959
William E. Colby (recording)	1900–1905	Charlotte E. Mauk	1959–

* Record of terms incomplete.

TREASURER

Mark B. Kerr, J. H. Senger,	Walter L. Huber 1931-1935
Warren Olney 1892–1896*	Francis P. Farquhar 1935-1936
J. H. Senger 1896-1898	Walter L. Huber 1936-1948
C. B. Bradley 1898-1899	Robert L. Lipman 1948-1950
Joseph N. LeConte..............1899-1915	Einar Nilsson 1950-1957
Marion R. Parsons 1915-1919	Richard M. Leonard.............1957-1959
Joseph N. LeConte 1919-1931	Clifford V. Heimbucher 1959–

FIFTH OFFICER

Ernest Dawson 1923–1925	Phil S. Bernays 1948–1949
William F. Badè..................1925–1927	David R. Brower...................1950–1953
Walter L. Huber..................1927–1931	Alexander Hildebrand 1953–1954
Duncan McDuffie 1931–1941	Joseph R. Momyer...............1954–1955
Lewis F. Clark........1941–1943, 1959–	Richard M. Leonard 1955–1957
Francis Farquhar 1943–1946, 1949–1950	Nathan C. Clark................1957–1958
William E. Colby 1946–1948	Charlotte E. Mauk..................1958–1959

ASSOCIATE SECRETARY

Holway R. Jones 1959–

EXECUTIVE DIRECTOR

David R. Brower...................................1953–

HONORARY PRESIDENT

Joseph N. LeConte (a charter member)............1931-1950
William E. Colby..1950–

HONORARY VICE-PRESIDENTS

George Davidson 1905-1911	Horace M. Albright 1937–
Robert Underwood Johnson....1905-1937	François E. Matthes..................1937-1948
David Starr Jordan 1905-1931	Robert M. Price..................1938-1940
Gifford Pinchot 1905-1912	Marion R. Parsons..................1938–1953
J. Horace McFarland 1912-1948	Duncan McDuffie 1941–1951
James Bryce 1912-1922	Newton B. Drury..................1942–
Henry S. Graves 1912-1920	Willis Linn Jepson..................1942–1946
Alexander G. McAdie 1913-1917	Joel H. Hildebrand 1943–
Enos A. Mills 1915-1920	Donald B. Tresidder..................1943–1948
Stephen T. Mather 1916-1930	Frederick Law Olmsted............1945–1957
Vernon L. Kellogg 1920-1937	Randall Henderson 1947–
William B. Greeley 1920-1937	Walter L. Huber..................1948–
John C. Merriam 1923-1945	Walter A. Starr 1948–
John Barton Payne 1923-1934	Francis P. Farquhar..................1951–
Ray Lyman Wilbur 1929-1949	Howard Zahniser 1952–
Robert G. Sproul 1933–	Phil S. Bernays..................1953–
William H. Wright..................1936–1959	Oliver Kehrlein 1958–

DIRECTORS

Until 1922 there were nine directors; since then fifteen, elected annually.

John Muir 1892-1914	William D. Armes ....1892- *
Warren Olney 1892-1909	J. Henry Senger 1892-1898
John C. Branner ....1892- *	Mark B. Kerr ....1892- *

* Record of terms incomplete.

David Starr Jordan 1892-1903
Willard D. Johnson ....1892- *
Robert M. Price ....1892 * ;
        1898-1900; 1915-1938
Joseph LeConte .... * -1898
Elliott McAllister .... * -1904
George Davidson .... * -1910
Cornelius B. Bradley .... * -1902
J. M. Stillman .... * -1898
Dorville Libby .... * -1896
W. R. Dudley 1898-1909
Joseph N. LeConte 1898-1940
Clarence L. Cory 1899-1901
Walter E. Magee 1899-1900
William E. Colby......................1900-1949
Warren Gregory 1902-1904
James S. Hutchinson 1903-1907
Alexander G. McAdie...............1904-1913
Edward T. Parsons 1904-1914
William F. Badè 1907-1936
E. C. Franklin........1909–1911, 1913–1914
Willoughby Rodman 1909-1915
William C. Morgan 1910-1912
Vernon L. Kellogg 1911-1920
Clair S. Tappaan 1912-1932
David P. Barrows 1914-1915
Marion R. Parsons 1914-1938
Charles P. Douglass 1915-1916
Walter L. Huber........................1915-1948
Albert H. Allen 1916-1919
Phil S. Bernays.........................1919–1953
Payson J. Treat 1920-1932
Edith Bridges 1922-1924
Ernest Dawson 1922–1925, 1926–1937
Aurelia S. Harwood 1922-1928
M. Hall McAllister 1922-1926
Duncan McDuffie, 1922–1923, 1925–1926,
        1928–1941, 1943–1946
Walter Mulford 1922–1923, 1925–1926
C. Nelson Hackett 1923-1924
Ralph Arthur Chase..................1924-1925
Francis P. Farquhar..................1924–1951
Charles J. Fox 1924-1925
William H. Wright 1925-1931
Herbert S. Adair....1926–1928, 1929–1935
Aurelia H. Reinhardt 1926-1927

Caroline E. Tracy 1927-1928
Chester H. Rowell 1928-1933
Edward Rainey 1931-1932
Virginia Best Adams 1932-1934
Francis D. Tappaan 1932-1943
D. Raymond Brothers 1932-1933
Mary Yost 1933-1935
Lewis F. Clark§...........................1933–
Ansel Adams 1934-
Bestor Robinson§ 1935–
Joel H. Hildebrand 1935–1943, 1945–1947
Samuel Merrill 1936-1937
Glen Dawson§ 1937–1951
Walter A. Starr 1937-1948
Oliver Kehrlein 1938-1958
Richard M. Leonard§ 1938–
E. Stanley Jones 1940–1941, 1943–1946
David R. Brower§ 1941–1953
Norman B. Livermore, Jr.§ 1941–1949
Leland Curtis 1943-1946
Charlotte E. Mauk 1943-
Harold E. Crowe 1943–1946, 1949–1959
Harriet T. Parsons 1943-1946
Arthur H. Blake....1943–1944, 1949–1952
Dean S. Curtis 1944-1945
Frank H. Lewis 1944-1945
Weldon F. Heald....1945–1946, 1947–1949
Alex Hildebrand 1948–1957
Robert L. Lipman......................1948-1950
H. Stewart Kimball 1949–1951, 1952–
Einar Nilsson 1950–1957
Harold C. Bradley......................1951–
Marjory B. Farquhar..................1951–1955
Arthur E. Johnson.....................1951–1954
Frank A. Kittredge.....................1953–1954
Joseph Momyer 1953–1956
A. Starker Leopold.....................1954–
Nathan C. Clark.........................1955–
Clifford Youngquist 1955–56, 1959–
Elmer C. Aldrich 1956–
William Siri 1956–
Lowell Sumner 1958–1959
Clifford V. Heimbucher 1959–
George Marshall 1959–

§In Armed Forces, 1943–1946.   * Record of term incomplete.

Editors of The Sierra Club Bulletin

J. Henry Senger, Chairman	1892–1894	(1:1–1:4)
Cornelius Beach Bradley	1895–1897	(1:5–2:5)
Warren Gregory	1898–1899	(2:3–2:6)
David Starr Jordan, Chairman	1900–1903	(3:1–4:3)
James S. Hutchinson, Jr.	1903–1904	(4:4–5:2)
Elliott McAllister	1905–1910	(5:3–7:4)
William Frederic Badè	1911–1922	(8:1–11:3)
C. Nelson Hackett	1923–1924	(11:4–12:1)
James S. Hutchinson, Jr.	1925	(12:2)
Francis P. Farquhar	1926–1946	(12:3–31:2)
David R. Brower	1946–1953	(31:3–38:8)
August Frugé, Chairman	1953–	(38:9–)

Chairmen of Club Committees

The names of the committees have not always been as shown. The Lodge Committee was first known as the LeConte Memorial Lodge Committee, and later as the LeConte and Parsons Lodge Committee. The Library Committee was first indicated only by the title, Librarian; Badè was actually chairman of a Committee on Archives. Visual-education was first conceived under the name Motion Picture Collection Committee. The succession of chairmen for Mountaineering presided over committees on registers, on nomenclature, on mountain records and place names. Conservation study was carried on by a Committee on Legislation in early years, and later by a National Park and Forest Policy Committee. The Natural Sciences Committee, once part of the Conservation Committee, became a separate committee encompassing glacier and bighorn studies once under separate committees.

OUTING

William E. Colby	1901-1937
Richard M. Leonard	1937-1942
Herbert L. Breed	1942-1946
Richard M. Leonard	1946–1951
H. Stewart Kimball	1951–

May Dornin	1933-1934
Louis N. Rice	1934-1936
Louise Hildebrand	1936-1937
Alfred E. Weiler	1938-1954
Mary Margaret Jones	1954-1958
William Siri	1958–

LODGES AND LANDS

E. T. Parsons	1905-1914
Marion Randall Parsons	1914-1917
J. N. LeConte	1917-1931
Peter J. Van Oosting	1931-1933
Lewis F. Clark	1933-1943
Arthur H. Blake	1943-1946
Alex Hildebrand	1946-1949
Richard N. Burnley	1949–1951
Lewis F. Clark	1951–1953
Laurence Burnley	1953–

MOUNTAINEERING

Oliver Kehrlein	1933-1934
Richard M. Leonard	1934-1936
Arthur H. Blake	1936-1940
David R. Brower	1940-1943
Arthur H. Blake	1943-1946
Raffi Bedayn	1946-1948
Morgan Harris	1948-1950
Allen P. Steck	1950-1953
Hervey Voge	1953-1956
Richard C. Houston	1956–

LIBRARY

Nell L. Taggard	1915-1918
Wallace Bradford	1918-1921
Francis P. Farquhar	1923-1924
W. F. Badè	1929-1930

TRAILS

Walter L. Huber	1929-1930
Walter A. Starr	1936–1941, 1946–
Arthur H. Blake	1941-1946

VISUAL EDUCATION

Nathan C. Clark 1933-1937
David R. Brower 1939-1943
Doris F. Leonard 1943-1947
Charlotte E. Mauk 1947-1948, 1953-1959
Kenneth D. Adam......................1948-1952
Wilbur Twining 1952-1953
Marjory Farquhar 1959–

WINTER SPORTS

Bestor Robinson 1932-1943
Richard H. Felter 1943-1946
Lewis F. Clark 1946-1948
Einar Nilsson 1948-1950
Alexander Hildebrand 1950–1951
John A. Linford 1951–

CONSERVATION

Walter A. Starr 1940-1941
Weldon F. Heald........................1945-1946
Arthur H. Blake........................1946-1951
Harold C. Bradley....................1951-1953
John R. Barnard........................1953–1955
Edgar Wayburn 1955–

MEMBERSHIP

E. W. Cunningham.....................**1947-1949**
Cicely M. Christy.......................1949–1953
Francis Whitaker 1953–1954
Kenneth D. Adam......................1954–

CLAIR TAPPAAN LODGE

Lewis F. Clark 1934–1943, 1947–1948
Richard N. Burnley **1943-1947**
James B. Clifford **1948-1950**
Richard N. Burnley...................1950–1951
James Mulholland 1951–1956
Robert McGillicuddy 1956–1959
Frank Shoemaker 1959–

NATURAL SCIENCES

Milton Hildebrand 1948–1953
A. Starker Leopold 1953–1955, 1957–1959
Richard D. Taber 1955–1956
William Graf 1956–1959
Lowell Sumner 1959–

PATRON MEMBERS

Abigail Avery
Harold C. Bradley
Mr. and Mrs. Stirling A. Colgate
E. T. Guymon, Jr.
Mr. and Mrs. D. Hanson Grubb
Helen M. and Joseph LeConte

Mrs. M. Hall McAllister
Mr. and Mrs. William Shand
Mr. and Mrs. Walter A. Starr
Russell and Dorothy Varian
Cedric and Rhea Wright

HONORARY LIFE MEMBERS

*Louis Bartlett
M. A. Benedict
Harold C. Bryant
Irving M. Clark
Arthur Connick
Arthur E. Demaray
William O. Douglas
Charles Eggert
C. M. Goethe
Jesse R. Hall
Herbert C. Jones

Alfred A. Knopf
E. P. Leavitt
Edward Mallinckrodt, Jr.
Lawrence C. Merriam
Helen Funk Muir
Olaus J. Murie
John B. Oakes
Nicholas Roosevelt
Carl P. Russell
John P. Saylor
Eivind T. Scoyen

S. B. Show
Wallace Stegner
Wallace Sterling
Perry A. Thompson
H. Bradford Washburn, Jr
Lyle F. Watts
Charles S. Webber
John R. White
Conrad Wirth
Walter A. Wood
Charles G. Woodbury

* Charter member.

Publications of the Sierra Club, 1892-1960

THE SIERRA CLUB BULLETIN

Publications marked with an asterisk are out of print in the original edition. Volumes 1–5 are available in reproduction by a photographic process. From 1928-1946 the magazine became one of six monthly numbers per volume; from 1947–1950, one of eleven; since 1951, one of ten. The indexing interval varies from two to four years. A 57-year index was published in 1952. The following are the semi-annual and annual numbers.

Publ.	Vol.	No.		Publ.	Vol.	No.	
2*	1	1	January, 1893	45		3	January, 1912
3*		2	June, 1893	46		4	June, 1912
6*		3	January, 1894	47	9	1	January, 1913
7*		4	May, 1894	48		2	June, 1913
9*		5	January, 1895	49*		3	January, 1914
10*		6	May, 1895	50		4	January, 1915
11*		7	January, 1896	51	10	1	January, 1916
13*		8	May, 1896	52		2	January, 1917
14*	2	1	January, 1897	53		3	January, 1918
15*		2	May, 1897	54		4	January, 1919
16*		3	January, 1898	55	11	1	January, 1920
17*		4	June, 1898	56		2	January, 1921
18*		5	January, 1899	57*		3	1922
19*		6	June, 1899	58*		4	1923
20*	3	1	January, 1900	59	12	1	1924
22*		2	May, 1900	60		2	1925
23*		3	February, 1901	61		3	1926
24*		4	June, 1901			4	1927
25*	4	1	January, 1902		13	1	1928
26*		2	June, 1902		14	1	1929
28*		3	February, 1903		15	1	1930
29*		4	June, 1903		16	1	1931
30*	5	1	January, 1904		17	1	1932
31*		2	June, 1904		18	1	1933
32*		3	January, 1905		19	3	1934
33*		4	June, 1905		20	1	1935
34	6	1	January, 1906		21	1	1936
35		2	January, 1907		22	1	1937
36		3	June, 1907		23	2	1938
37		4	January, 1908		24	3	1939
38		5	June, 1908		25	1	1940
39	7	1	January, 1909		26	1	1941
40		2	June, 1909		27	4	1942
41		3	January, 1910		28	3	1943
42		4	June, 1910		29	5	1944
43	8	1	January, 1911		30	6	1945
44		2	June, 1911		31	6	1946

Publ.	Vol.		Publ.	Vol.	
32	5	1947	39	6	1954
33	3	1948	40	8	1955
34	6	1949	41	10	1956
35	6	1950	42	6	1957
36	5	1951	43	9	1958
37	10	1952	44	7	1959
38	8	1953			

OTHER PUBLICATIONS

1* Articles of Association, By-Laws, and List of Members. 1892.

4* Maps of a Portion of the Sierra Nevada Adjacent to the Yosemite.
    (J. N. Le Conte.) 1893.

5* Map of a Portion of the Sierra Nevada Adjacent to the Kings River.
    (J. N. Le Conte.) 1893.

8* Table of Elevations within the Pacific Coast.
    (Mark B. Kerr and R. H. Chapman.) 1895.

12* Map of the Central Portion of the Sierra Nevada Mountains and of the Yosemite
    Valley. (J. N. Le Conte.) 1896.

21* Ramblings Through the High Sierra. By Joseph Le Conte. Reprinted from SCB,
    1900; issued as separate, 1900.

27* A Flora of the South Fork of Kings River. By Alice Eastwood. 1903.

62* Place Names of the High Sierra. By Francis P. Farquhar. 1926.

A Journal of Ramblings Through the High Sierra of California by the University
    Excursion Party. By Joseph Le Conte. 1930, 1960.

Manual of Ski Mountaineering. Edited by David R. Brower. 1942, revised 1946, 1947
    (Univ. Calif. Press) ; 1960.

John Muir's Studies in the Sierra.* Introduction by William E. Colby.
    Foreword by John P. Buwalda. 1950, 1960.

Sierra Club Bulletin. Vols. 1–5, 1893–1905. Reprinted by offset. Cloth bound.
    $32.50 per set of 5. 1950.

Guide to the John Muir Trail. By Walter A. Starr, Jr.
    With a Map of the Sierra Nevada, 1934, 1943, 1946, 1951, 1953, 1956, 1959.

The Sierra Club: A Handbook. Edited by David R. Brower. Initially published as
    SCB, 32:10, 1947; revised, 1951, 1955, 1957, 1960.

Fifty-seven-year Index to the Sierra Club Bulletin (1893–1949). 1952.

Going Light—With Backpack or Burro. Edited by David R. Brower. Illustrated by
    Milton Hildebrand. 1951, 1952, 1954, 1956, 1958.

A Climber's Guide to the High Sierra. Edited by Hervey Voge. 1954, 1956.

Wilderness River Trail. By Charles Eggert. 28 minutes, color and sound. 1954.
    (23 copies.)

This Is Dinosaur: Echo Park Country and Its Magic Rivers. Edited by Wallace
    Stegner. (Knopf.) 1955.

Two Yosemites. By David Brower. 10 minutes, color and sound. 1955. (15 copies.)

A Climber's Guide to Pinnacles National Monument. By David Hammack.
    1955, 1960.

Belaying the Leader: An Omnibus on Climbing Safety. By Richard M. Leonard et al.
    1956, 1959.

A Climber's Guide to the Teton Range. By Leigh Ortenburger.
    Illustrated by Eldon N. Dye. 1956.
Wilderness Alps of Stehekin. By David Brower. 31 minutes, color and sound. 1958.
    (51 copies.)
The Mammoth Lakes Sierra: A Handbook for Roadside and Trail.
    Edited by Genny Schumacher. August, October, 1959.
Wilderness Cards from the Sierra Club: Nos. 1–12, 1959; nos. 13–15, 1960.
This Is the American Earth. By Ansel Adams and Nancy Newhall. 1960.
Portfolio III: Yosemite. By Ansel Adams. 1960.
The Meaning of Wilderness to Science. Edited by David Brower. 1960.

Periodicals in the Library

ADIRONDACK MOUNTAIN CLUB, Albany, N.Y. *The Ad-i-ron-dac.* (Bi-monthly.)

ALPINE CLUB, London, England. *The Alpine Journal.* (Semiannual.)

ALPINE CLUB OF CANADA, Vancouver, B.C. *Avalanche Echoes.* (Monthly.) *The Canadian Alpine Journal.* (Annual.)

ALPINE SPORT CLUB, INC., Auckland, New Zealand. *Alpinesport.* (Quarterly.)

AMERICAN ALPINE CLUB, New York. N.Y. *The American Alpine Journal.* (Annual.)

AMERICAN FORESTRY ASSOCIATION, Washington, D.C. *American Forests.* (Monthly.)

AMERICAN MUSEUM OF NATURAL HISTORY, New York, N.Y. *Natural History.* (Monthly.)

AMERICAN PLANNING AND CIVIC ASSOCIATION, Washington, D.C. *American Planning and Civic Annual. Planning and Civic Comment.* (Quarterly.)

APPALACHIAN MOUNTAIN CLUB, Boston, Mass. *Bulletin.* (Monthly.) *Appalachia.* (Semiannual.)

APPALACHIAN TRAIL CONFERENCE, INC., Washington, D.C. *Appalachian Trailway News.* (Quarterly.)

AUTOMOBILE CLUB OF SOUTHERN CALIFORNIA, Beverly Hills, Calif. *Westways.* (Monthly.)

BERKELEY HIKING CLUB, Berkeley, Calif. *Hobnail.* (Monthly.)

BRITISH COLUMBIA MOUNTAINEERING CLUB, Vancouver, B.C. *The B. C. Mountaineer.* (Monthly.)

BRITISH GLACIOLOGICAL SOCIETY, London, England. *The Journal of Glaciology.* (Semiannual.)

BRITISH MOUNTAINEERING COUNCIL, London, England. *Mountaineering.* (Monthly.)

CALIFORNIA ACADEMY OF SCIENCES, San Francisco, Calif. *Pacific Discovery.* (Bi-Monthly.)

CALIFORNIA ALPINE CLUB, San Francisco, Calif. *Trails.* (Monthly.)

CALIFORNIA HISTORICAL SOCIETY, San Francisco, Calif. *Quarterly.*

CENTRO EXCURSIONISTA DE CATALIÑA, Barcelona, Spain. *Montaña.* (Quarterly.)

CHEMEKETANS, Salem, Ore. *The Chemeketan.* (Monthly.)

THE CLIMBERS' CLUB, London, England. *The Climbers' Club Journal.* (Annual.)

CLUB ALPIN BELGE, Bruxelles, Belgium. *Revue Alpine.* (Monthly.)

CLUB ALPIN FRANÇAIS, SECTION LYONNAISE, Lyons, France. *Revue Alpine.* (Monthly.)

CLUB ALPINE FRANÇAIS ET GROUPE DE HAUTE MONTAGNE, Paris, France. *La Montagne et Alpinisme.* (Monthly.)

CLUB ALPINO ITALIANO. Sezione di Milano, Milano, Italy. *Bollettino Mensile.* (Monthly.)

CLUB ALPINO ITALIANO, Torino, Italy. *Revista Mensile.* (Monthly.)

CLUB DE EXPLORACIONES DE MEXICO, Mexico City. *La Montaña.* (Monthly.)

COLORADO GAME AND FISH DEPT., Denver. *Colorado Conservation.* (Monthly.)

COLORADO MOUNTAIN CLUB, Denver, Colo. *Trail and Timberline.* (Monthly.)

CONTRA COSTA HILLS CLUB, Oakland, Calif. *Knapsack.* (Monthly.)

DESERT PUBLISHING COMPANY, El Centro, Calif. *Desert Magazine.* (Monthly.)

DEUTSCHEN ALPENVEREINS, Munich, Germany. *Mitteilungen.* (Monthly.)

DIVISION OF FORESTRY, STATE DEPARTMENT OF NATURAL RESOURCES, Sacramento, Calif. *News Letter.* (Monthly.)

DU GROUPE DE HAUTE MONTAGNE, Paris, France. *Annales du Groupe de Haute Montagne.* (Annual.)

EVERGLADES NATURAL HISTORY ASSOCIATION, Homestead, Florida. *Everglades Natural History.* (Quarterly.)

EXPLORERS CLUB, New York, N.Y. *The Explorers Journal.* (Quarterly.)

FEDERATION OF WESTERN OUTDOOR CLUBS, *Western Outdoor Quarterly.*

GREEN MOUNTAIN CLUB, INC., Middlebury, Vt. *The Long Trail News.* (Quarterly.)

HAWAIIAN TRAIL AND MOUNTAIN CLUB, Honolulu. *Bulletin.* (Monthly.)

HIMALAYAN CLUB, Calcutta, India. *Himalayan Journal.* (Annual.)

JAPANESE ALPINE CLUB, Tokyo, Japan. *Alpinist.* (Monthly.)

LANE PUBLISHING COMPANY, Menlo Park, Calif. *Sunset Magazine.* (Monthly.)

MAZAMAS, Portland, Ore. *Mazama.* (Monthly.)

MOUNT BAKER HIKING CLUB, Bellingham, Wash. *The Rambler.* (Bi-monthly.)

MOUNTAIN CLUB OF MARYLAND, INC., Baltimore, Md. *MCM Bulletin.* (Quarterly.)

THE MOUNTAINEERING ASSOCIATION, London, England. *Mountain Craft.* (Quarterly.)

MOUNTAINEERING CLUB OF SOUTH AFRICA, Cape Town Section, Cape Town, South Africa. *Journal of the Mountain Club of South Africa.* (Annual.)

MOUNTAINEERS, Seattle, Wash. *The Mountaineer.* (Monthly.)

NATIONAL AUDUBON SOCIETY, New York, N.Y. *Audubon Magazine.* (Bi-monthly.)

NATIONAL PARKS ASSOCIATION, Washington, D.C. *National Parks Bulletin.* (Quarterly.)

NEW ZEALAND ALPINE CLUB, New Zealand. *New Zealand Alpine Journal.* (Annual.)

OBSIDIANS, INC., Eugene, Ore. *The Obsidian.* (Monthly.)

OLYMPIC MOUNTAINEERS, Port Angeles, Wash. *Klahhane Club.* (Monthly.)

OREGON STATE COLLEGE MOUNTAIN CLUB, Corvallis, Ore. *Local Yodel.* (Monthly.)

ÖSTERREICHISCHER ALPENVEREIN, Innsbruck, Austria. *Der Bergsteiger.* (Monthly.)

POTOMAC APPALACHIAN TRAIL CLUB, Washington, D.C. *Bulletin.* (Quarterly.) Also *Up Rope.* (Monthly.)

PRAIRIE CLUB, Chicago, Ill. *Bulletin.* (Monthly.) *Year Book.*

SCHWEIZER ALPENCLUB (CLUB ALPIN SUISSE, CLUB ALPINO SVIZZERO), Bern, Switzerland. *Die Alpen - Les Alpes - Le Alpi.* (Monthly.)

SCOTTISH MOUNTAINEERING CLUB, Edinburgh, Scotland. *The Scottish Mountaineering Journal.* (Annual.)

SIERRA CLUB, San Francisco, Calif. *Sierra Club Bulletin.* (Monthly.)

SIERRA CLUB, ANGELES CHAPTER, Los Angeles, Calif. *Southern Sierran.* (Monthly.)

SIERRA CLUB, ATLANTIC CHAPTER, New York, N.Y. *The Argonaut.* (Occasional.)

SIERRA CLUB, KERN-KAWEAH CHAPTER, Bakersfield, Calif. *Kern-Kaweah Newsletter.* (Monthly.)

SIERRA CLUB, LOMA PRIETA CHAPTER, San Jose, Calif. *The Loma Prietan.* (Monthly.)

SIERRA CLUB, LOS PADRES CHAPTER, Santa Barbara, Calif. *Condor Call.* (Monthly.)

SIERRA CLUB, MOTHER LODE CHAPTER, Sacramento, Calif. *The Bonanza.* (Monthly.)

SIERRA CLUB, *Pacific Northwest Chapter Newsletter.*

SIERRA CLUB, RIVERSIDE CHAPTER, Riverside, Calif. *Palm & Pine.* (Monthly.)

SIERRA CLUB, SAN DIEGO CHAPTER, San Diego, Calif. *Hi Sierrans.* (Monthly.)

SIERRA CLUB, SAN FRANCISCO BAY CHAPTER, San Francisco, Calif. *Sierra Club Yodeler.* (Bi-weekly.)

SIERRA CLUB, SAN FRANCISCO BAY CHAPTER, NATURAL SCIENCE SECTION, San Francisco, Calif. *Sierra Club Nature Notes.*

SIERRA CLUB, SKI MOUNTAINEERS & ROCK CLIMBING SECTIONS, Los Angeles, Calif. *Mugelnoos.* (Monthly.)

SIERRA CLUB, TEHIPITE CHAPTER, Fresno, Calif. *Tehipite Topics.* (Monthly.)

Summit Magazine. Big Bear Lake, Calif. (Monthly.)

SWISS FOUNDATION FOR ALPINE RESEARCH, Zurich, Switzerland. *Journal.*

TAMALPAIS CONSERVATION CLUB, San Francisco, Calif. *California Out-of-Doors.* (Triennial.)

TARARUA TRAMPING CLUB, Wellington, N.Z. *The Tararua Tramper.* (Monthly.)

TRAILS CLUB, Portland, Ore. *The Trail Blazer.* (Monthly.)

U. S. NATIONAL PARK SERVICE, Washington, D.C. *Annual Report of the Director.*

WASHINGTON ROCK CLIMBERS, Washington, D.C. *Up Rope.* (Bi-weekly.)

WILDERNESS SOCIETY, Washington, D.C. *The Living Wilderness.* (Quarterly.)

WYOMING GAME AND FISH COMMISSION, Cheyenne, Wyoming, Wyoming Wild Life. (Monthly.)

YOSEMITE NATURAL HISTORY ASSOCIATION, Yosemite, Calif. *Yosemite Nature Notes.* (Monthly.)

YUGOSLAV MOUNTAINEERING CLUB, Likozarjeva, Yugoslavia. *Planinski Vestnik.*

By-Laws of the Sierra Club

ARTICLE I.—*Name*

The name of this corporation shall be the SIERRA CLUB.

ARTICLE II.—*Purposes*

The purposes for which this corporation is formed are as follows:

To explore, enjoy, and preserve the Sierra Nevada and other scenic resources of the United States and its forests, waters, wildlife, and wilderness; to undertake and to publish scientific, literary, and educational studies concerning them; to educate the people with regard to the national and state forests, parks, monuments, and other natural resources of especial scenic beauty and to enlist public interest and coöperation in protecting them.

ARTICLE III.—*Place of Business*

The place where the principal business of said corporation is to be transacted is the City and County of San Francisco, State of California.

[*The foregoing articles, forming part of the articles of incorporation (see page 117), can be changed only by amending such articles as provided by law.*]

ARTICLE IV.—*Directors and Officers*

SECTION 1. The government of the club shall be entrusted to fifteen of its members to be known as the Board of Directors who shall elect from their number a president and vice-president and who shall elect from the club membership a secretary and a treasurer who, if not members of the board, shall become ex officio members.

SECTION 2. The Directors shall enter upon their term of office on the first Saturday in May following their election and shall thereupon elect the officers specified, who shall be the officers of the club as well as of the board, and such officers shall hold office for one year and until their successors are elected and have qualified.

Each director shall be elected for a term of three (3) years and five (5) directors shall be elected by the membership at each annual election.

SECTION 3. The Board of Directors shall be the managing board of the club, control the election of the members of the club, control all expenditures and property of the club, fill vacancies in the board and its officers, and act for its interests in any way not inconsistent with these by-laws; but shall have no power to subject the club to any liability beyond the amount of the corporate funds.

ARTICLE V.—*President*

The president shall preside at all meetings of the club and of the Board of Directors; enforce the by-laws; call such meetings as he is empowered to call; nominate all standing committees, of each of which he shall be *ex officio* a member, said nominations to be presented to the Board of Directors for confirmation at the commencement of his term of office; exercise general supervision over the affairs of the club; and have such other powers as ordinarily accompany the office.

ARTICLE VI.—*Vice-President*

During the absence or disability of the president the vice-president shall act in his place; and in case both president and vice-president are absent from any meeting, the secretary shall call the meeting to order, and an acting president be elected by the meeting.

ARTICLE VII.—*Secretary*

The secretary shall keep an exact record of the proceedings of the club and of the Board of Directors; have charge of the records of the club; give notice to the members or the directors, as the case may be, of meetings of the club and of the board; shall receive and receipt for the dues and other moneys belonging to the club, and deposit the same, in the name of the club, with the bank or banks designated by the Board of Directors; submit names of persons recommended for membership in the club as hereinafter provided; submit to the members, to be voted on, such questions as may be certified to him by the Board of Directors for that purpose; and annually, and at such other times as may be required, present to the Board of Directors reports upon the membership of the club and upon its activities.

ARTICLE VIII.—*Treasurer*

The treasurer shall, under the general supervision of the Board of Directors, have custody of the moneys and investments belonging to the club; make disbursements and investments of the club's funds in accordance with regulations prescribed by the Board of Directors; keep proper books of account; and annually, and at such other times as may be required, submit to the Board of Directors a report of receipts and disbursements and the financial condition of the club.

ARTICLE IX.—*Honorary Officers*

SECTION 1. The Board of Directors may, at its discretion elect annually by unanimous vote an Honorary President who shall have preëminently distinguished himself in furthering the purposes of the club.

SECTION 2. The board may also elect annually, by unanimous vote, honorary vice-presidents, selected because of conspicuous services rendered in furtherance of the purposes of the club, or because of some material assistance they may have rendered the club.

SECTION 3. The honorary president and the honorary vice-presidents, upon election to the respective offices, shall be *ipso facto* members of the club and shall have all the privileges of members, but during the terms for which they are elected they shall be exempt from the payment of dues.

ARTICLE X (a).—*Executive Committee*

SECTION 1. An Executive Committee, consisting of the president, the vice-president, and three other members of the Board of Directors chosen by the Board, shall have power to act for the Board of Directors in case of emergency or when it is impracticable to convene the Board.

SECTION 2. The Executive Committee shall serve as a committee on finances, on legislation, and on public relations, and on such other matters as the Board of Directors may specifically delegate to it.

ARTICLE X *(b)—Sierra Club Council*

Section 1. The Sierra Club Council shall be composed as follows: (a) one representative appointed by each committee authorized by the Board of Directors to appoint a representative; (b) one representative appointed by the executive committee of each chapter.

Each representative shall serve at the will of the appointing committee and each such committee is authorized to appoint an alternate representative to serve in the absence of its representative.

SECTION 2. No Director shall be eligible to serve as a member of the Council.

SECTION 3. The Council shall have power to recommend to the Board of Directors or apropriate committee on any matter affecting the club and to act upon matters delegated to it by the Board of Directors.

SECTION 4. The Council shall have power to elect a chairman and other officers and to establish its own rules of procedure.

ARTICLE XI.—*Standing Committees*

The Board of Directors may create and appoint such standing or special and advisory committees as it may from time to time deem necessary for the promotion and proper conduct of the objectives of the club. All members of the club shall be eligible to membership upon all committees so created.

ARTICLE XII.—*Chapters*

SECTION 1. Members of the club who reside in the same region may, with the approval of the Board of Directors, form a chapter of the Sierra Club. No chapter shall be approved unless an application signed by at least fifty members of the club in good standing, all residents of the designated region, shall have been filed with the board. The application shall state the proposed boundaries of the region and the name chosen by the applicants. If the proposed boundaries include territory already assigned to an existing chapter the application must be accompanied by a waiver duly authorized by said chapter.

SECTION 2. As soon as the formation of a chapter has been approved by the Board of Directors, the secretary of the club shall send a notice to all members of the club who reside in the designated territory inviting them to attend a meeting for the purpose of organizing the chapter, and in said notice shall name three of the members who signed the application as temporary chairman, first vice-chairman, and second vice-chairman, respectively.

SECTION 3. At its organization meeting a chapter shall adopt by-laws and elect an executive committee to manage its affairs. The by-laws of a chapter shall not contain anything which is at variance with the expressed purposes of the club or its by-laws, and shall be approved by the directors before becoming effective. A chapter may not change its name, its boundaries, or its by-laws without the approval of the directors.

SECTION 4. The Board of Directors may suspend or annul a chapter if at any time its membership falls below fifty or if, in the opinion of the board, such action is for the best interests of the club; but such action shall not affect the standing of the individual members as members of the club. The Board of Directors shall not suspend or annul a chapter, however, until after written specifications of the ground or grounds upon which the proposed action is to be based shall have been furnished to the principal officer or officers of the chapter involved, and a reasonable opportunity allowed such chapter to present evidence in opposition to the proposed action and affording it a full opportunity to be heard thereon. The affirmative vote of at least nine directors shall be required to carry a motion to annul or suspend a chapter.

SECTION 5. Any member of the club who resides within the territorial limits of a chapter shall be considered to be a member of that chapter and shall be entitled to all its privileges. No member of the club shall belong to more than one chapter. Any member of the club who (*a*) resides in territory in which there is no chapter, or (*b*) resides within the boundaries of one chapter but desires membership in another chapter, may, upon written application to the secretary of the club, become a member of the chapter of his choice.

SECTION 6. No dues shall be assessed or collected by a chapter. Each chapter shall be entitled to receive from the treasurer of the club an amount determined by the Board of Directors, not greater than twenty-five per cent of the amount collected as regular dues from the members of the respective chapter. In determining these amounts each chapter shall be considered separately. Such amounts shall be payable to the treasurers of the respective chapters quarterly as collected. Nothing in this section shall, however, prevent the Board of Directors from allotting funds to chapters for specific purposes.

SECTION 7. Chapters shall not own real estate; but the Board of Directors may place the management of any of the club's property in the hands of a chapter. All members of the club shall, however, have equal privileges on the club's property.

SECTION 8. Each chapter is authorized to undertake all such local activities within its own territory as are not inconsistent with the purposes of the club and are not prohibited by the Board of Directors by a general rule applicable alike to all chapters. Chapters shall not act on questions of public policy without the consent of the Board of Directors, except to recommend action by the Board of Directors, or to secure from it permission to take such action as the chapter may desire.

SECTION 9. Chapters shall not conduct outings of more than ten days' duration without the express consent of the Board of Directors.

ARTICLE XIII.—*Nomination of Directors*

SECTION 1. The Board of Directors shall, at least two months before the annual election, provide for the appointment of five members of the club, no one of whom shall be a director, to constitute a Nominating Committee; and two members of the club as alternates. It shall be the duty of this committee to nominate for directors for the ensuing term at least seven candidates. The name of any member proposed in writing to the committee by any fifty members of the club shall be added to the ticket. All members of the club in good standing are eligible for nomination. Six weeks before the annual election the Nominating Committee shall file its report with the secretary of the club, the names arranged in an order determined by lot. A ballot containing the names of the nominees in the order presented by the Nominating Committee shall be printed and mailed to each member of the club at least four weeks before the date of election. This ballot shall have two blank spaces for convenient insertion of additional names.

SECTION 2. The Nominating Committee may at its own discretion, or shall at the request of the Board of Directors, prepare a brief statement concerning each nominee, and these statements shall be printed and enclosed with the ballots.

ARTICLE XIV.—*Election of Directors*

SECTION 1. The annual election for directors shall be held on the second Saturday of April of each year, and the voting shall be by secret ballot. The polls shall close at 12 o'clock noon on the day of election. A plurality of votes shall elect.

SECTION 2. The Board of Directors shall provide for the appointment from the membership of the club of nine Judges of Election, and a number of alternates, to supervise said election, and it shall be their duty to count the ballots and tabulate the results and report to the president and secretary in writing the number of votes cast for each candidate and the names of those elected to serve as directors. The secretary shall thereupon notify in writing the members elected.

ARTICLE XV.—*Removal from Office*

Any director or other officer of the club may be removed from office for good cause shown, by a three-fourths vote of all ballots cast at a special vote of the club as provided for in Article XXII.

ARTICLE XVI.—*Meetings of the Board of Directors*

SECTION 1. Meetings of the Board of Directors shall be held when called by the president or by five members of the board. The secretary shall mail to each member of the board a written notice specifying the time and place of meeting at least two days prior thereto. A majority of the directors shall constitute a quorum and form a board for the transaction of business.

SECTION 2. All meetings of the Board of Directors or of any executive committee or other committee thereof, shall be open to attendance by any member of the club in good standing, but nothing herein shall prevent the Board of Directors or any such committee, by resolution or other appropriate action, convening in private session for the consideration of any matter which may come before them, but the vote or other final action of such board or committee shall be taken in open session.

ARTICLE XVII.—*Annual Dues*

SECTION 1. The annual dues of all members excepting as specified elsewhere in these by-laws shall be seven dollars payable in advance on April 1, for the fiscal year ending March 31, following.

SECTION 2. The husband or wife of a member may become a member in full standing upon payment of the regular admission fee and annual dues of one-half of the rate of regular members.

Such members shall not receive the publications and special mailings which are sent out by the club.

SECTION 3. The annual dues for members who are under the age of 21 years on each April 1 shall be one-half of the rate of regular members.

SECTION 4. The Board of Directors shall establish an admission fee.

SECTION 5. Newly elected members whose applications are filed between April first and August thirty-first shall pay the annual dues for the current fiscal year. Newly elected members whose applications are filed between September first and December thirty-first shall pay fifty per cent as dues for the current fiscal year. Newly elected members whose applications are filed between January first and March thirty-first shall pay the annual dues for the ensuing fiscal year.

SECTION 6. On or about April first of each year the secretary shall send out notices of dues. All members whose dues are unpaid on June first shall be notified of impending suspension of membership effective June thirtieth, and shall be suspended on that date if not paid before then. Members whose dues are unpaid on October thirty-first shall thereupon cease to be members.

SECTION 7. Former members who have been dropped for nonpayment of dues may be reinstated at the discretion of the Executive Committee.

SECTION 8. The Executive Committee may cancel or remit, in whole or in part, the dues of a member without other record than a written notice to the secretary signed by the president or the vice-president.

SECTION 9. Any member or applicant may become a life member, or a member of any other classification established by the Board of Directors, upon payment of a fee set by the Board; said fee shall not be less than dues for regular members, except as otherwise provided in these by-laws.

SECTION 10. One dollar out of the annual dues of each member shall be considered as subscription to the Sierra Club Bulletin. The subscriptions of members not paying dues shall be considered as having been paid for out of other unappropriated income.

ARTICLE XVIII.—*Permanent Fund*

All moneys received for life memberships and such other sums as may be received or appropriated by the Board of Directors for permanent investment shall be securely and separately invested as a permanent fund, the income only of which shall be expended.

ARTICLE XIX.—*Membership*

SECTION 1. The membership of the club shall consist of persons twelve years of age or over who are interested in advancing the purposes of the club.

SECTION 2. All applications for membership shall be addressed to the secretary of the club at its principal office. Each application shall be accompanied by the admission fee and dues prescribed in Article XVII. Applications shall be in writing and shall be signed by the applicant, and shall contain a statement that the applicant is aware of the purposes of the club and desires to support them.

SECTION 3. Each applicant shall be sponsored by one member of the club in good standing and more than 21 years of age who has been a member for at least one year.

SECTION 4. Within fifteen days after receiving an application, the secretary of the club shall notify the membership committee thereof and the membership committee of the chapter within whose area the applicant resides. If no protest is received by the club membership committee within thirty days thereafter the applicant shall be elected to membership; provided, however, that the Board of Directors is empowered to extend the time within which protests may be filed. In all other cases the club membership committee, by majority vote, shall take action on the application.

SECTION 5. Honorary members may be elected by unanimous vote of the Board of Directors present at a meeting, for life or for specified terms. Honorary members shall be exempt from dues and from admission fees.

ARTICLE XX.—*Resignation of Members*

SECTION 1. All resignations must be made in writing to the Board of Directors.

SECTION 2. No resignation of membership shall be accepted or take effect until all indebtedness to the club shall have been paid by the resigning member.

SECTION 3. All privileges to use any of the property of the club and all rights and privileges as a member of the club of such resigning members, or of any member ceasing to be such by dismissal, death, or any other cause, shall cease upon the termination of membership.

ARTICLE XXI.—*Discipline*

SECTION 1. Any member may be suspended or expelled by a vote of at least nine members of the Board of Directors, but no such vote shall be taken until after the member and the executive committee of the chapter, if any, to which said member belongs, shall have been furnished with a statement of the charges preferred against him, and shall have been given at least one week's notice of the time when the same will be considered by the board; and every member shall have the right to appear before the board, and be heard in answer to the charges, before final action thereon shall be taken.

SECTION 2. Any chapter, through its executive committee, shall have the right to file charges against any member of the club and such member shall thereupon be automatically suspended from participation in all activities of the club until the directors shall take action upon the charges preferred as hereinbefore provided.

ARTICLE XXII.—*Ballot by the Club*

Whenever the Board of Directors shall decide that any question submitted to it for its decision is of such importance that it should be submitted to a vote of the members of the club, the board shall cause to be certified to the secretary the form in which such question shall be submitted and shall direct him to have such question printed on the regular ballot for directors; or, if it should order a special vote to be taken on the question, the secretary shall thereupon prepare a special ballot with such question printed thereon, and the mailing of such ballot and the canvass of the vote on such questions shall be conducted in all other respects in the same manner as the annual election of directors is conducted. A majority vote of all the ballots cast shall decide the question. The board shall, upon the written request of fifty members of the club, submit to a vote such question as they may propose.

ARTICLE XXIII.—*Construction of By-Laws*

On all questions as to the construction or meaning of the by-laws and rules of the club, the decision of the Board of Directors shall be final, unless rescinded by the club by vote as provided for in the preceding article.

ARTICLE XXIV.—*Amendments to By-Laws*

SECTION 1. These by-laws are fundamental, and shall not be altered, amended, suspended, or repealed, in whole or in part, except by a two-thirds vote of all the ballots cast at any annual or special election, which ballots shall be so printed as to enable the members voting to express their wish as to the adoption or rejection of any proposed amendment or alteration. Such proposed amendment or alteration must be printed in full, and mailed to each member with his ballot, and shall only be submitted to a vote of the club when presented in the manner indicated in Article XXII.

ARTICLES OF INCORPORATION

Know All Men by These Presents:

That we, the undersigned, a majority of whom are citizens and residents of the State of California, have this day voluntarily associated ourselves together for the purpose of forming a corporation under the laws of the State of California.

And we hereby certify as follows, to wit:

I. That the name of said Corporation shall be the *Sierra Club.*

II. That the said Association is made and the said Corporation is formed, not for pecuniary profit. No part of the assets or net earnings of this corporation shall be distributed to or shall inure to the benefit of any member, officer or director; provided, however, that payment of reasonable compensation for services rendered and expenses incurred may be made.

III. That the purposes for which this corporation is formed are as follows:

To explore, enjoy, and preserve the Sierra Nevada and other scenic resources of the United States and its forests, waters, wildlife, and wilderness; to undertake and to publish scientific, literary, and educational studies concerning them; to educate the people with regard to the national and state forests, parks, monuments, and other natural resources of especial scenic beauty and to enlist public interest and cooperation in protecting them.

IV. That the place where the principal business of said corporation is to be transacted is the City and County of San Francisco, State of California.

V. That this corporation shall have perpetual existence.

VI. That the number of Directors of said corporation shall be 15; provided, however, that the number of Directors may be changed by the By-Laws from time to time, but there shall be not less than 3 nor more than 25 Directors.

The Directors who are appointed for the first year, to serve until the election and qualification of their successors, are as follows:

John Muir, Martinez
Warren Olney, Oakland
J. H. Senger, San Francisco
Wm. D. Armes, Oakland

David S. Jordan, Palo Alto
R. M. Price, Berkeley
Mark Brickell Kerr, Golden Gate
Willard D. Johnson, Berkeley

John C. Branner, Palo Alto

VII. That the said Corporation has and shall have, no Capital Stock.

And we further certify and declare: That the above-named Directors of the Corporation were duly elected Directors thereof by the members of said Corporation, at an election for Directors held at #101 Sansome Street in the City and County of San Francisco, State of California, at eleven A.M. on this 4th day of June, 1892, and that a majority of the members of said Association and Corporation were present and voted at said election, and that at such election each of the said Directors received the votes of a majority of the members of the Corporation present at such election; as more fully appears from the Certificate of the two Tellers of Election hereunto annexed and hereby referred to and made a part hereof.

In Witness Whereof, we have hereunto set our hands and seals this 4th day of June, A.D. 1892.

W. H. Beatty
Ralph C. Harrison
George C. Perkins
G. B. Bayley
C. B. Bradley
Hermann Kower

Fred S. Pheby
Hubert P. Dyer
Charles G. Harker
W. H. Henry
R. M. Price
L. de F. Bartlett

Will Denman
W. L. Jepson, Jr.
Warren Gregory
Warren Olney
John Muir
J. H. Senger

THE SIERRA CLUB

..s	Dorville Libby	Willard D. Johnson
..ll Kerr	James O. Griffin	C. D. Robinson
..anner	Charles A. Bailey	Josiah Keep

California,
..d County of San Francisco } ss.

..n this fourth day of June, A.D. 1892, before me, Alfred A. Enquist, a Notary ..ic in and for said City and County of San Francisco, State of California, duly ..mmissioned and sworn, personally appeared W. H. Beatty, Ralph C. Harrison, ..o. C. Perkins, John Muir, J. H. Senger, Wm. D. Armes, Mark Brickell Kerr, John .. Branner, Dorville Libby, James O. Griffin, Charles A. Bailey, Willard D. Johnson, C. D. Robinson, Josiah Keep, C. B. Bradley, Hermann Kower, Fred S. Pheby, Hubert P. Dyer, Charles G. Harker, W. H. Henry, R. M. Price, L. de F. Bartlett, Will Denman, W. L. Jepson, Jr., Warren Gregory, Warren Olney and G. B. Bayley, known to me to be the persons whose names are subscribed to and who executed the within instrument and they acknowledged to me that they executed the same.

In Witness Whereof, I have hereunto set my hand and affixed my Official Seal, the day and year last above written.
(Notarial Seal)

ALFRED A. ENQUIST,
Notary Public in and for the City
and County of San Francisco.

State of California,
City and County of San Francisco } ss.

We, the undersigned, L. de F. Bartlett and Hermann Kower, being first duly sworn, depose and say:

That a meeting of the Members and Incorporators of the *Sierra Club* was duly held at the hour of 11 A.M. on said June 4th, 1892, at #101 Sansome Street, in the City and County of San Francisco, State of California; that at said meeting an election of Directors of the said Corporation was duly held by the members thereof, and that a majority of the members of said Association or Corporation were present at said meeting and voted at said election. That we, the undersigned, were duly appointed at said meeting to be the Tellers and Judges of the said election, and that we duly canvassed and reported the ballots cast at said election for the Directors of said Corporation, and that each of the Nine (9) Directors of said Corporation mentioned in the foregoing Articles of Incorporation (which are hereby referred to and made a part of this affidavit) received the vote of a majority of the members of the said Corporation voting at said election, and received a larger vote than was received by any other person who was voted for at said election, as a Director; and that said nine persons thereby became and are the duly elected Directors of the said Corporation.

In witness whereof we have hereunto set our hands and seals this 4th day of June, A.D. 1892.

L. de F. Bartlett (Seal)
Hermann Kower (Seal)

Subscribed and sworn to before me this 4th day of June, A.D. 1892.

(Seal)

ALFRED A. ENQUIST,
Notary Public in and for the City and County
of San Francisco, State of California.